Explore the Power of Astrolo[gy]

Trikona

An advanced approach to the three vital houses of the chart

Dr. Ambika Prasad Parashar
Dr. Vinod Kumar Parashar

UNICORN BOOKS

Publishers
UNICORN BOOKS, New Delhi-110002
E-mail: unicornbooks@vsnl.com
Website: www.unicornbooks.in • www.kidscorner.in

Distributors
Pustak Mahal, Delhi
J-3/16 , Daryaganj, New Delhi-110002
☎ 23276539, 23272783, 23272784 • *Fax:* 011-23260518
E-mail: info@pustakmahal.com
Website: www.pustakmahal.com

London Office
5, Roddell Court, Bath Road, Slough SL3 OQJ, England
E-mail: pustakmahaluk@pustakmahal.com

Sales Centre
10-B, Netaji Subhash Marg, Daryaganj, New Delhi-110002
☎ 23268292, 23268293, 23279900 • *Fax:* 011-23280567
E-mail: rapidexdelhi@indiatimes.com

Branch Offices
Bangalore: ☎ 22234025
E-mail: pmblr@sancharnet.in • pustak@sancharnet.in
Mumbai: ☎ 22010941
E-mail: rapidex@bom5.vsnl.net.in
Patna: ☎ 3294193 • *Telefax:* 0612-2302719
E-mail: rapidexptn@rediffmail.com
Hyderabad: *Telefax:* 040-24737290
E-mail: pustakmahalhyd@yahoo.co.in

ISBN 978-81-7806-108-5

Edition : 2007

Printed at : Param Offsetters, Okhla, New Delhi-110020

Dedicated To

The entire management and the staff of
Pustak Mahal/Unicorn Books for their
perpetual devotion and hard work
directed to educate the common
person of our country.

Acknowledgement

The authors thankfully acknowledge the help and facilities provided by Sanjaya Parashar, the youngest son of Dr. A. P. Parashar, in completing this work. The authors also gratefully acknowledge immense material help provided by the Brazoria County Library, Angleton, in Taxes, USA, that enabled them to complete this uncommon project on astrology. The authors are also thankful to the members of their family who directly or indirectly inspired them to complete this work. They are also immensely grateful to the numberless readers, who read their first book on astrology—**Explore the Power of Astrology**—and send inspiring e-mails conveying their appreciation. They authors feel indebted to the established and renowned astrologers both within the country and outside for their inspiring and enlightening material related to the astrological knowledge, which enriched their insight and enabled them to produce this work.

Contents

Preface

In fact, *Jotish* or traditional Indian astrology is extremely complex and is different in many ways from Western astrology. It depends on knowing one's exact time and place of birth to make a correct chart (*kundali*) which may help you to predict events of your life correctly. (2: p. xxii) You may be quite familiar with the Sun signs but the Sun signs are just the beginnings of the process. All the twelve signs appear somewhere in your own birth chart and in addition to the Sun, the Moon, Jupiter, Mercury, Venus and other planets also appear in the chart somewhere. Based on the date, place and time of your birth, the signs in the houses create your astrological birth chart (*kundali*), which tells more about yourself and about your life. It tells all about you, your personality, your likes and dislikes, your romance, your children, your spouse, your creativity, job opportunities, the areas of jobs where you will better succeed, your finances, and your social status etc.

In fact, astrology can explain all of that. Planets can show the various energies at work in your life and the signs demonstrate how these energies behave in your birth chart. The houses are where the various areas of your life disclose, from your family life, romance, financial affluence to your higher education and foreign travel, etc. Trikona is an earnest attempt in this direction. Truly speaking, this time we have chosen three most important houses of the chart— ***the first house***, which is also known as the ascendant or the house of self, personality, likes and dislikes, ***the ninth house***, known as the house of luck, foreign travels and higher education, and ***the fifth house***, known as the house of children, creativity, and romance. *Surprisingly, these three houses can predict most of your life's big and important events hence they are very important houses astrologically*. However, there are other houses which form similar Trikonas and relate to the other areas of your life. For example, the third house, seventh house and the eleventh house also form a Trikona and relate about your brothers and sisters, friends, partner and social status as well as gains. But **Trikona** we have dealt with in this book contains most important areas of your life. Hence a detailed treatment is given to them in **Trikona** for the benefit of the interested reader. Although we have presented elaborate explanations on all the twelve houses in our first book, **Explore the Power of Astrology, Trikona** is an advanced approach to the three very vital houses, which unfold much more than what we normally know about them.

We hope that **Trikona** will prove to be a guide to the very important areas of your life that have been left undiscovered so far. If our humble attempt inspires you, and you believe that you have learnt more about astrology, we shall feel rewarded. We have discussed thirty-six charts in all the three areas of Trikona to present good examples that unfold the movements and placements of the various planets, telling and explaining what the planets can bring you if placed in the three houses known as Trikona. We very much hope that the book will not only be rewarding but also entertaining.

APP
VKP
e-mail: ap_98607@yahoo.co.in

✡ CHAPTER ONE ✡

The Trikona

Does Astrology work?

Many people don't care a bit what astrology is or what it can really do? But there are hundreds who do believe that it can do wonders and can help solving personal or any kind of problems. They also hold that it can show them some way to reach their goals. Well, does astrology really work is a thousand dollar question? The astrologers of the past had a motto, which they reflected boldly in their books on astrology. "The stars incline, they do not compel." In other words under the influence of the planets, one may feel tired but that planetary influence cannot force one to drive a car or make one fell asleep while driving a car.

In fact, people believe in astrology for more than 3000 years. But they are quite capable of believing something silly for thousand years, until they are proven wrong. Even if they are proven wrong, some of them will go on believing their silly theories. Yes, it is a proven fact that astrology works, but not the way most people think it does. Perhaps it is the biggest mistake of the people to reckon that astrology can do impossible—like foretelling someone's future very accurately. The ancient Indian astrologers did have a great depth in this respect as they were able to foretell one's future to a great extent, but at the same time there are examples from the legends that cast doubt on that sort of belief. Many events that took place in Sri Ram's life happened unexpectedly although the great saga Vishwamitra was one of the leading astrologers and the guru of the day and astrology was also quite rampant during those days.

Still astrology works. Not by telling you what is actually going to happen as it is not that simple to tell, but by indicating what possibly may happen. No sane astrologer will claim that he or she can foretell everything very accurately about one's future. Even then astrology works. It works within simple limits. There may be plenty of arguments about just how clearly astrology can see into the future, but there is no doubt about one simple fact that any good astrologer can see something. A practising astrologer can tell you when you will feel particularly romantic or when you may be careless enough to meet an accident or even when you will have very hard times relating to your finances or family. Roughly, one can also calculate what shall be one's peak years of life or even when one may get married or when possibly one's death (*markesh yoga*) may occur.

Truly speaking there is practically no area in which astrology cannot be helpful. There is no area of life to which astrology cannot be usefully applied to—starting from birth right through one's retirement. It would not be true to state that wherever human life is, so also astrology. As you go through this book, you will gradually be more convinced of that. Since we are mainly concentrating on the *trikonas* in this book, we will primarily deal with the matters relating to the three houses or angles we call Trikona. These three angles or houses are the first house or **the ascendant, the fifth house** and **the ninth house.** The reader may get confused to identify which is the fifth or the ninth house in a chart. Traditionally, Indian astrologers reckon the houses anti-clockwise. Therefore, the house, which is counted as the fifth from the ascendant, is the fifth house whereas the house counted as the ninth from the ascendant, is considered to be the ninth house.

We implore the reader to read our previous book on astrology—-**Explore the Power of Astrology**. It is not only very informative and throws light on various unsolved astrological matters, but it also helps one to understand the basics which are highly imperative to learn astrology from the beginning. The current effort is a stepping stone to enlightening the reader and to make him/her understand certain important astrological matters relating to **the three houses** that can bestow beneficial or devastating effects on a person subject to the placement of their owners in a chart (*kundali*). We shall analyze a good number of charts for the benefit of the reader after we have discussed the characteristics and effects of these three houses separately. But before we begin our discussions on the *trikonas,* we would like the reader to understand the nature and importance of the **12 zodiac rising signs** to which certain major qualities are associated. When the Sun enters these zodiac signs after each month, it does take those qualities.

In fact, the Sun is the most powerful planet astrologically as it actually bestows different characteristics in an individual. When the Sun transits different zodiac signs, it governs different characteristics. Therefore, the position of the Sun in a birth chart governs one's individuality, distinctive style and the drives to fulfil one's goals. J. M. Woolfolk reckons that your horoscope is a painting of you. The characteristics of your Sun sign are the broad strokes that the artist first lays down on the canvas. The artist outlines your general shape, the planes and the angles of your face, the way in which you hold your body. In the same manner the Sun signs determine your general character. How do you deal with your responsibility? Are you easy going or persistently follow the life's goals? Answers of many of these questions may be found to a great extent in your Sun sign. (8: pp.3-4)

The Twelve Zodiac Signs

Since ancient times astrologers in India always recognized 12 zodiac signs. During the past few centuries in the West astrologers have also recognized 12 familiar zodiac signs through which all the planets march past. We now look at how the zodiac signs are identified and associated with certain major personal characteristics. Long time ago, the star constellations that lie behind 30-degree segments of the zodiac were given the names they now have because the star patterns were thought to look like those figures. 'Through the centuries, however, and because of irregularity in the Earth's revolution on its axis as it revolves around the Sun, the sky that the ancients observed has "shifted."

In fact, the fixed stars (constellation) that the zodiac signs are named after have moved slowly backward in the sky. It has a process called the "precession of the equinoxes." The stars have moved so much that the zodiac signs are no longer in their original constellation.' (10: p.54)

The following table contains the names and the figures of the 12 zodiac signs that represent different characteristics astrologically.

TABLE 1:12

Zodiac Signs with their names & figures

Aries

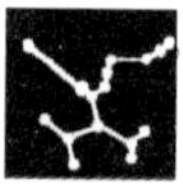

Taurus

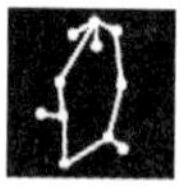

Gemini

Cancer

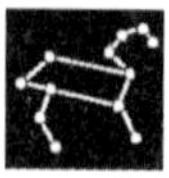

Leo

Virgo

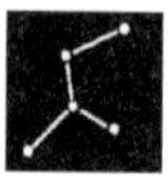

Libra

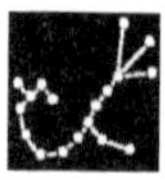

Scorpio

Sagittarius

Capricorn

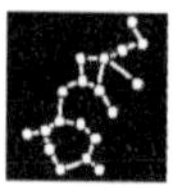

Aquarius

Pisces

The dates reflected under each zodiac sign correspond to the Indian astrological system only. The Western system slightly differs from it in that respect.

ARIES *(Mesa)* **: the Ram**
April 14—May 13

Prominent Characteristics

Aries is the first sign of the zodiac. It symbolizes new beginnings. It signifies quick changes and sudden forks in the road. Aries' life is marked by arriving at a certain place and then being turned in a new direction. Certainly one can say that an Aries' life is adventurous. There is a dynamic restlessness in Aries' life. One born with the Sun in Aries becomes an activist and a doer. Outwardly an Aries appears to be talkative, vibrant and exciting. Most Aries people are direct, outspoken and uncomplicated. Such natives are greatly exciting and demonstrative. They are generous to a fault and at times oddly affectionate. (6: p.12) An Aries is a natural leader, who possesses great confidence. The native is very generous about helping others. He/she is a natural-born warrior, fearless and courageous. An Aries subject is warm and ardent in human relationships. There is nothing half- hearted in that kind of individual. In fact, independence is a key word of an Aries, who is willing to take a gamble, follow a dream, set the mind on a goal, and pursue it with overwhelming enthusiasm. Optimism is his/her supreme quality, but some times an Aries lacks tact and diplomacy. (8: p.9-10)

An Aries person can become a good executive, police officer, fire fighter, film stunt person, ambulance driver, film director, soldier, sales representative, iron or steel worker, an athlete, a racing driver and a circus performer. (6: p.14) Briefly, an Aries is energetic, assertive, urgent, strong -minded, quick, straightforward, enthusiastic, selfish, possesses initiative, impulsive, fiery, mostly positive and outgoing in nature, adventurous, possesses a sense of self-respect, high energy levels, fast-paced life style, highly competitive, enjoys taking risks, hot- headed and rude, regardless of obstacles, energetic, and determined to fulfil the work in his/her own way. (10: p.55)

TAURUS (*Vrashaba*) **: the Bull**

May 14—June 13

Prominent Characteristics

One born with the sign Taurus is likely to persevere when others fall by wayside. Because perseverance is a characteristic most required for success, a Taurus person tends to be successful. The greatest strength of a Taurus resides in firmness and steady drive. He/she is a purposeful achiever who possesses endless patience to see a thing through and to make it a success. A Taurus person is most comfortable with the familiar environment and situations. Often a Taurus individual is patient but it is only when opposed that he/she becomes angry. However, unless someone seriously provokes the Taurus, he/she is gentle and loves to sit to smell the flower. A Taurus person is quiet and gentle but the native knows his/her own mind and, therefore, nothing can dissuade him/her when once convinced that he/she is on the right track. Fortunately, this sign possesses a lot of firmness and usually is strong enough, physically and mentally to overcome most of the life's obstacles. Born in Taurus sign a person is often caring, giving and affectionate and have a great liking for all things beautiful. He/she is endowed with genuine creative gifts and is highly inspired by art and music.(8: p.13)

A Taurus born individual can be a farmer, construction worker, forest ranger, domestic worker, cook, stockbroker, accountant, financial adviser, architect, works in theaters, painter, hotelier, bank manager, musician, singer, teacher, dress designer. (6: p.18) Briefly, a Taurus person is possessive, reliable, loyal, stubborn, sturdy, lazy, patent; persistent; romantic, charming, affectionate, warm, beautiful, sincere, self-indulgent, confidence inspiring, luxury and comfort loving, obsessive possessiveness, artistic in taste and nature, and slow to get angry but when aroused can be fearsome.

GEMINI (*Mithuna*) : **the Twins**

June 14—July 13-14

Prominent Characteristics

People born with the sign Gemini are many-sided, quick in thought and action, clever with words, quite skilful at handling others and full of new ideas. Most astrologers consider Gemini as a human sign because it seems to possess qualities that are distinguishing characteristics of human race, such as, intelligence, adaptability, and communicativeness. People born in Gemini sign quite often excel in professions related to teaching, law and politics. They enjoy as actors, journalists, telesales, dancers and entertainers; love modelling, acrobat, oratory, and are very happy in jobs like airport workers, railroad contactors and travel consultants. (6: p.22) They enjoy writing and chatting with people. A Gemini individual is highly persuasive and can quickly pick up information here and gossip there. This makes him/her an ideal conversationalist. His/her gifts of writing, speaking and self-expression makes it a success in dealing with the public. A Gemini can adapt to many kinds of situations and deal with different sorts of people. As a Gemini individual is highly amusing, versatile and witty, he/she can lift people out of their problems. A Gemini always tries not to dampen his/her high spirits. Such a person has a wide range of good contacts used when needed. Change is Gemini's key word and he/she values freedom most. (8: p.18-19)

In fact, Gemini people need mental challenges to keep them busy on the job and it cannot be the same challenge over and over again. Carriers like advertising, writing, broadcasting, and public relations often appeal to them besides what we have said already. A Gemini possesses an inquiring mind and is a good sales person too. With his/her wit and communication, a Gemini is excellent in persuading others. (4: p.66) Briefly, a Gemini is versatile, communicative, witty, intellectual, sharp, restless, lively, quick-witted, detest boredom, sharing emotional & intellectual energies in a variety of undertakings, ability to do several things at a time, philosophical, tendency not to settle down with one thing or person, often skips over the important details, yet quite responsible and reliable to an extent. (10: p.57)

CANCER ***(kerka)*** **: the Crab**

July 14—August 13-14

Prominent Characteristics

A person born with Cancer sign may appear gentle, kind and sympathetic. Astrologers also hold that more than any other sign a Cancer born person is a series of contradiction. Often a person with Cancer sign may be complex, fragile, unpredictable, temperamental, and may need constant support and encouragement. Such a native wants desperately to be loved and approved of. His/her greatest impact is in human relationship. The native is very cautious about revealing too much of oneself. He/she guards the secrets very well. A Cancer born native is very possessive. Anyone who becomes part of his/her life will never again be free. The native is artistic and creative and has formidable intellectual talents. A Cancer born individual is generally loyal, hardworking, unafraid of menial tasks, but he/she does not enjoy performing extraneous tasks. Such people possess an instinct for business combined with imagination that is quite magical for acquiring financial security. The native never gets enough love and approval for he/she always needs more. If you would a Cancer born person he/she will never forget it and will carry grudges for life.(4: p.68)

Prominent Cancer occupations would be hotelier, caterer, business executive, accountant, financial adviser, welfare officer, sailor, antique collector, real estate agent, teacher, jeweller, and waitress. Briefly a Cancer born individual is protective, sensitive, emotional, imaginative, moody, loving, creative, artistically gifted, most challenging to get to know and learn, overtly hard but internally cool and reserved, underneath highly emotional and sensitive, can look withdrawn, greatly compassionate, intuitive, protective of the family and home, make loyal parent, abides by the rule to a great extent, love justice, honest to a considerable extent, loves swimming, diving, ice-skating, boating, rowing, rifle-shooting, playing cricket, surfing and enjoys water polo as well.

LEO : *(Simha)*

August 14—September 13-14

Prominent Characteristics

A Leo born native's most likeable traits or qualities are excitement, liveliness and high spirits. The native is devoted to the self. Most Leos possess a kingdom, which may be small or big but he/she is the ruler of that kingdom. A Leo person possesses self-assurance. At a party or gathering a Leo person assumes control of the occasion. A Leo person is a fluent talker and a born entertainer who can make every occasion a happy event. Because by nature a Leo individual is showy and expensive, he/she dislikes the ordinary and the dull. When in reality there is less excitement, he/she would try to create it. When the native invites people to his/her place, they are very lavishly and honestly entertained. A Leo individual wants to enjoy the good life without minding what it costs to him/her. The public image is very important for a Leo- born individual. Leos are the most plentiful spenders among all the people of the zodiac. If approached in the right way, Leo people are the best friends. A Leo person is highly egoistic who demands more adoration than respect. The Leo native is an order-giver rather than an order-taker. But at times a Leo individual is also lazy and indolent. (8: p.26-27)

As Leo is a fixed sign, Leo individuals may be determined, stubborn, habit-bound but very confident to lead. They are proud, courageous, and self-assured to a fault. The native is often generous, commanding and ambitious, but he/she can also be intolerant, demanding and self-righteous. As a Leo's memories are short, he/she is quick to forgive.(4: p.73) Briefly, a Leo person is often bossy, expensive, generous, loving, creative, impressive, natural leaders, intensely enthusiastic, generous, magnanimous with the charm, fiercely proud and confident, love and live life to its fullest, magnificently affectionate, dramatic, creative, dislikes small mindedness and meanness, very dogmatic, often stubborn, autocratic, unbending but often forgiving too. He/she loves to adhere to the rule. He/she is pompous, is theatrical, fun-loving, sportsman, runner, love aerobics, polo player, wrestler, weight-lifter, yoga lover, football-player, affectionate and egocentric. The occupations that a Leo person may love to follow are: acting, modelling, fashion designing, company executive, directing films, fire fighting, animal training, and likes becoming police official, musician, even jewellery maker. (6: p.30)

VIRGO : *(Kannya)*

September 15—October13

Prominent Characteristics

The planet Mercury rules both Gemini and Virgo, as such, it inspires its subjects towards constant activity. It drives the Virgo born subjects to ceaseless drive to accomplish and perfect. The native will not postpone any work for tomorrow and will like to finish it today, if it is possible. Such a subject is organized and is not a daydreamer but a day-doer. Such subjects possess a great capacity for love but love is not enough for them to be happy. The Virgo subject is ambitious, but not just for money. He/she will want to know more to attain wisdom and to use it to practical uses. Such a native is never happy to cheat others. He/she is very intelligent, possesses excellent memory, analytical mind, and is known for clear thinking. The native can look into human minds and has the ability to prove into human motivations. People like to consult such a subject for various problems and take advice before putting their plans into action. Such subjects don't like ideas without facts as they distrust vague ideas. As Virgo is a changeable sign, the native can adjust easily to the change once, if he/she finds a way of fitting the new situation into the routine. A Virgo person's nature is shy and reserved. He/she always prefers small company to converse with, as at such occasions he/she can offer the best in him/her. At times the Virgo subjects' highly refined way of analyzing things may make them unhappy for they want perfection. A warm and loving relationship may bring out the best in such a subject because basically he/she is kind and loyal. (8: p.30-31)

In brief, a Virgo is modest, analytical, critical, painstaking, fussy, intelligent, sharp, foresighted, judicious, hardworking, worrying, small-minded, practical to a great extent, restless, diligent, capable, warm and loving, quick thinking, possesses excess mental energy, subject to tension and stress, desires for perfection and inclines to be over critical at times. The planet Mercury rules Gemini and Virgo so the native is quite persuasive in communication, always keen to win arguments and people, and also represents innocence with justice. (10: p.60) Virgo often loves to choose occupations of a secretary, filing clerk, nurse, welfare officer, architect, estimator, banker, accountant, domestic help, writer, computer operator, nutritionist, therapist, teacher, philosopher and legal advisors. (6: p.34) Many Virgin subjects like to go to the health field and to the jobs that require analysis, including marketing, system analysis and love to stay in detail-oriented jobs. Being great lovers of beauty they have a great understanding of botany and like botany-related jobs.

LIBRA : *(Tula)*

October 14—November 13

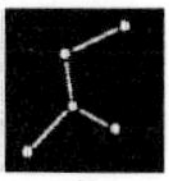

Prominent Characteristics

Libra subjects are social people who like to share their experience with others. They are quick to form partnerships and friendships. They are friendly, popular, attractive, and like to talk about their high principles and lofty ideals. Libra subjects are always happy in finding balance in other things, not merely in human relationships.

As Libras are highly romantic, they are always in search of an ideal mate. But often such a desire gets unfulfilled and it brings disappointments to the native. (4: p.84) Libra subject is easy to be liked for he/she possesses a captivating charm, and is usually beautiful to look at. Librans are born charmers and possess a gift to making others feel important. Flowers, jewellery, and lovely surroundings are the objects of a Libra person's life. The native is at his/her best in personal relationships. As a Libra person is born under the sign of Scales, he/she strives for balance and harmony and is happiest when the surrounding environment is serene and ordered. It also tends to depict a Libran to be shaky and indecisive. Librans are often born diplomats. A Libran is affectionate, warm-hearted, sentimental, naturally optimistic and, therefore, tries hard at everything to please others. However, underneath the friendly exterior, a Libran always longs for love and approval. (8: p.36)

Briefly a Libran is sociable, diplomatic, angry and aggrieved, charming, easygoing, polite, well-balanced, refined, cool, romantic, impractical, self-seeking, well-read, warm-hearted, out-going, concerned with achieving balance, harmony and peace. He/she loves justice around and easy communication. He/she is clever, persuasive, frank to a considerable extent, is often known as lazy, good at peacekeeping types of jobs, artistic in nature, music lover and reconciling. Libra occupations are: florist, librarian, fashion designer, publisher, journalist, artist, air steward, musician, hair-dresser, beauty consultant, judge, lawyer, counsellor, media personal, actor, secretary, clerk, and sometimes accountant. (6: p.38)

SCORPIO : *(Virshika)*

November 14—December 13-14

Prominent Characteristics

The Scorpio people are considered to possess extremes. They are variously identified as powerful, weak, independent, passionate, cold and a bundle of contradictions consisting of the best and the worst as well in human nature. A Scorpio subject possesses great intensity and would never like to do half-heartedly. Such a native lives on many levels. He/she may look calm and smiling at the surface, but ferocious, extremely strong-willed and determined inside. At times the native is also flexible when solutions are worked out, but if failed in any adventure, he/she would not accept defeat easily. The subject is extremely agile. As the native always has some hidden agenda, he/she may be misunderstood many times. Though the native may look at ease and relaxed, but such a subject will always be evaluating and working out plans to succeed. A Scorpio subject never forgets an act of kindness and tries to repay it profusely. He/she will also not forgive an injury and may wait for years to repay it. Many times the subject is revengeful too. Scorpios are most clever with money and like to amass wealth, as they don't like spending it. A Scorpio person is very passionate in love and emotional about everything in which he/she becomes involved. (8: p.40-41)

Briefly, a Scorpion individual is magnetic, passionate, intense, intuitive, possessive, shrewd, intuitive, penetrating, determined, jealous, obsessive, sexually infatuated, intensively private, great achiever and possesses ability to overcome challenging situations and obstacles, values his intimate relationship and friendship, works hard to exploit the best in those he adores, easily hurt and responds adversely at times, scientific in outlook, loves to finish the game he is involved. A Scorpio person may choose occupations to become a stockbroker, private detective, police officer, gynaecologist, surgeon, midwife, company director, army officer, psychiatrist, lifeguard, architect, actor, and a farmer. (6: p.42)

SAGITTARIUS : *(Danus)*
December 14—January 13

Prominent Characteristics

The sign Sagittarius is ruled by Jupiter, so the subject is full of life. Astrologers believe that a Sagittarius person has the gift from the providence that luck always protects him/her in work, friendship, career and money. Naturally, it affects the native's disposition, which is mostly cheerful. A Sagittarius person is full of enthusiasm, restlessness and joviality. The subject is very progressive, adventurous, and loves constant change of scene. The native's restless inquiring nature requires travel, excitement and to get what is unconventional or untraditional. Like the sign, the Sagittarius individual is always in search for wisdom. The subject tends to be an explorer who always loves philosophical pursuits. A Sagittarius person is always a good friend, who is openhearted, kind, jovial, totally free of malice and ready to help others.

The native loves freedom most. His/her passion for liberty underlies all other qualities. As far possible the subject does not meddle in others' affairs, and is not jealous of others. The native possesses a great sense of humor, has a wide range of interests, such as, music, nature, philosophy computer technology, theatre; he/she is versatile, imaginative, clever and ready to accept what is untraditional. (8: p.45-46)

Briefly, a Sagittarius person is outspoken, optimistic, philosophical, chatty, intellectual, freedom-seeking, quick-tempered, inconsistant, challenge-loving, humorous, lively, bound with boundless energy, explorative, tactless adventurous, interested in intellectual as well as physical pursuits, versatile in nature, combines wisdom and bravery, affectionate, extrovert, often appreciated by those whom he encounters, kind, implicit with knowledge, undertakes sacrifices for others, loves sports such as archery, horse riding, hockey, shooting, football, baseball shooting, etc. However, the occupations a Sagittarius person likes, are: sales representative, truck or cab driver, travel representative, jockey, comedian, entertainer, story writer, army officer, sports-related jobs, teacher and professor. (6: p.46-48)

CAPRICORN : *(Makar)*
January 14—February 13

Prominent Characteristics

Most Capricorns are ambitious and their lives are spent in the purposeful pursuits of their destiny. Their motivational force is desire for success, money, status, authority, position, and for obtaining love. A Capricorn individual's personality is implicit with practicality and initiative geared towards attaining leadership and power. Like the Capricorn symbol goat, which is a born climber to the top, the native always tries hard to reach the top. The Capricorn native always carries with the knowledge that there are tasks to be fulfilled. Such a native possesses a great sense of the value of time, which helps him/her to become a great organizer and planner. The subject is endowed with the sense of responsibility, discipline and restriction. The native is ambitious, practical and determined. He/she is highly diligent, creative and has little time for idle pleasure. Essentially, the subject feels that he/she can depend only on the self. Such a native is often misunderstood by others for looking cold to others, but it is because of his/her being sober nature that he/she looks like that. The subject is certainly cautious and conservative with money. Such an individual is not comfortable with ambiguity and tends to see things clearly. A Capricorn native is hard to be understood for he/she often bears a mask that covers him/her from being discovered. To others the native may appear aloof, indifferent and hard to reach, because he/she is often so self-contained. But his/her loyalty and affections run deep and protect those whom he/she loves. (8: p.50-52)

Briefly, the native is ambitious, prudent, practical, calculative, disciplined, and possesses two distinct nature. One is hard working, enterprising, highly motivated, setting high achieveable goals of life and loving life; the other side is to be lost in an imagined world, at times, cannot find enough motivation to take action, possesses a tendency to complain about imagined burdens, which may lead Capricorns to love solitude and to become introvert in nature. A Capricorn native is sensible, reserved, cautious, hard-working, reliable, cold, insecure, wise, moralistic, sensual, dutiful, and loves to work as a judge, lawyer, high-ranking police officer, prison officer, bank executive, engineer, sales executive, secretary, auto mechanic, shopkeeper, teacher, actor, cultivator and a military officer. (6: p.50)

AQUARIUS : *(Kumbha)*

February 14—March 13

Prominent Characteristics

An Aquarius individual will find anything out of ordinary interests. Such individuals are either at times eccentric individuals or crazy inventors. Like the Water Bearer's fixed sign the native represents persistent development of the intellect through communication and planetary influence. Aquarians will often be progressive and open-minded but that also lead them to be fixed in their opinions. The native is idealistic, inventive, original and may look easily aloof, detached or even cranky. But the native has a human connection and does not care for the human divisions created by humans themselves. An Aquarian would believe in, "I love humankind. It's people I can't stand."

The native's strongest trait or quality is the intellectual independence. Such a native can easily excel in professions in which creativity is needed. It is not limited to the arts either, but can extend to scientific innovations as well as inventions, to public service or civil rights reforms or even to owning a business. One, who takes to marketing, will have unique ideas. There is also a pretty good chance for the native to work in media. In spite of the field an Aquarian works, one can count on him/her having created solutions to the problems others thought insoluble. (4: p.102-103) Aquarians may also like to choose jobs as pilots, airport-workers, electricity workers and electric engineers, scientists, astronomers, astrologers, brain surgeons, psychiatrists, computer operators, entertainers, gynaecologists, film directors and actors. (6: p.35) As Aquarius is a sign of future and of a visionary, astrologers are found to be born under this sign. Uranus (traditionally Saturn) being the owner of the sign, creates a personality which is liberal, progressive at the same time fixed in opinion. The native's character is endowed with paradoxes; he/she enjoys being with the people but happy to be alone, loves travelling but feels relaxed to be at home. The subject possesses both a scientific and artistic turn of mind. Natives born under this sign live most intensely in their minds. Such a native is gifted to deal with all kinds of personalities from every walk of life. The subject's nicest part of the character is that he/she never indulges in judging others and likes to give this opportunity to others to do it. Ultimately, the subject loves freedom of opinion and to stay free in thinking. (8: p.55-56)

Briefly, an Aquarian is humane, independent, detached, original, honest, inventive, fiercely individualistic and independent intellectual, rarely forms permanent relationship with anyone, cool, aloof, noted to be friendly, kind, helpful, caring, possesses deep humanitarian instincts. Essentially, they are typically private people, possess originality and creativity. They are gifted with inventiveness, equally comfortable working in dissimilar worlds, such as, social work and science. They are possessive of great knowledge, unemotional, self-opinionated, magnetic and unique. (10: p.65)

PISCES : *(Meena)*

March 14—April 13

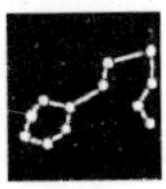

Prominent Characteristics

Most astrologers in the West reckon that Pisces is a sign that represent eternity, reincarnation and spiritual rebirth. Pisceans seem to possess other worldly qualities—mystically being described as possessing half-body and half-spirit. Thus, pulled between material and spiritual existence, possessed of the knowledge with which he/she will never be entirely at home in the real world. The native is in possession of the insight with which he/she is able to see deeply into the human psyche. The native possesses great intuitive powers with which he/she can foresee things happen. Such natives have extreme sympathy for people who are hurt, animals that are hungry and plants that are sick. Such a native can hardly say 'no' to anyone who is in need. At times such subjects are lazy, careless and emotionally confused. Therefore, the native needs to develop a positive self-image and ability to take responsibility. Since Pisces is a mystical sign of the zodiac, the native could be a good poet or a dreamer and can be a good writer, musician or an artist. As a Pisces person is blended with compassion and understanding, he/she exerts a unique power on people whose lives are greatly connected with him/her. The native may feel lack of confidence as a leader, but he/she is certainly a guide, teacher and a role model to many. (8: p.60-61)

Briefly such a native is rich in imagination, intuitive, sensitive, vague, dual-natured, compassionate, easily persuaded, sensual, emotional, rich in imagination, creative dreamer, and a poet. Pisceans are often divided into two extremes—one, wanting to do something real and valuable in the world they live and the other, moody, self-sacrificing, at times confused, dependent, retreating to their private world of imagination and dreams. Because of their dual nature they are often prone to extreme nervous tension and even escapism. At times they lack self-confidence and are unable to get on with the real world; minus this inability they are finest human beings who are not only good artists but are also great humanitarians.

Piscean likes to become a musician, artist, poet, pharmacist, service engineer, coastguard, fisherman, plumber, oil-rig worker, sailor, nurse, social worker, chemist, counsellor, teacher, soothsayer, forecast teller, and even an astrologer (6: p.58). Pisceans are sports adoring people who love surfing, playing football, ice-skating, water rafting, gymnastics, swimming and playing cricket.

✡ CHAPTER TWO ✡

The Ascendant

The House of Self

The ascendant is the house of self. It is the house where one's personality and self-image reside. Here is the house where one will find one's personal style from one's mannerism to temperament, from one's disposition to likes and dislikes. This house also includes one's physical body and early childhood and is tied with one's health too. If the house is successfully analyzed, it will also unfold one's sense of control and direction.

We have broadly listed in the first chapter the main characteristics of the Zodiac Signs, which considerably affect human conduct and behavior. Both the Sun and the ascendant rising in a chart at birth bestow on an individual these characteristics to a considerable extent. We have already discussed in our previous book, **Explore the Power of Astrology**, how to determine the ascendant at the time of birth as most events in an individual's life are hooked to it to a significant extent. Since we are limiting our discussion in this book only to the three angles called, **Trikonas**, we shall now proceed to discuss matters relating to the ascendant. The first angle (*trikona*), commonly known as the **ascendant** or **the rising sign** or ***lagna***, is the first *trikona*, which is determined in a chart or horoscope in view of the rising zodiac sign in the horizon at the time of individual's birth. We shall provide a simple example of calculating one's ascendant at the time of birth once again for the reader's reference.*

Ascertaining the Ascendant

Everyday each zodiac sign also rises in the East in the morning in line with the Sun sign. For example, if the Sun enters the sign Aries on April 14 at 5.45 AM, the zodiac sign Aries will also rise at the same time in the horizon that day and will roughly continue for two hours until 7.45 AM. After that the sign Taurus will rise in the horizon for next two hours. Therefore, if one is born on April 14 at 7.50 AM his/her ascendant will be Taurus as at that time the sign Taurus was rising in the horizon although the Sun still continues in the sign Aries in which it will continue until May 13. Thus, all the 12 zodiac signs rotate in 24 hours in the horizon (each zodiac sign continues rising roughly for two hours only) but the Sun continues rising in the same sign each day for one month.

The reader must keep in mind that the zodiac sign that rises with the Sun on the first day of its new sign will appear 4 minutes earlier in the horizon on the next day. For example, on April 15, the zodiac sign Aries will rise at 5.41 AM and will continue until 7.41 AM only.** Although it looks slightly complicated, but a good thinking done patiently would solve the reader's problem to comprehend ascertaining **the rising sign** in a chart. If once it is understood correctly, it will be easy to place the remaining planets in a chart with the help of a good Hindi calendar (*punchang*).

---

* Please read Chapter two in our book, **Explore the Power of Astrology**, Published by Unicorn Publishing Co., New Delhi to find out how to determine the ascendant at the time of one's birth.

** We would like the reader to consult a good Hindi *Punchang* (calendar) to ascertain the ascendant correctly.

The Strength of the Ascendant

The ascendant in a chart is a very important angle to determine the entire personality structure of a person. It is a great astrological factor which is extremely important to understand the nature of one's personality, behavior, motivation, physical strength, urge to pursue goals in life, and the amount of success one would get. Julia and Derek Parker hold: "In the past, astrologers believed that the Sun sign revealed the "secret you" known only by those closest to you. In contrast, the rising sign was believed to reveal the "public you," the image you presented to the world. Today, we believe the reverse is true: your Sun sign influences your public image; the rising sign indicates the "inner you." Considering together, both signs reveal a picture of who you are, inside and out."(10: p.70)

We reckon, Julia and Derek Parker are right to a great extent as the both, **the Sun sign** and **the rising sign** certainly determine the conduct, physical strength, motivations, strength of character, tastes, eating habits, one's gait, style of working, even what profession one is likely to choose, and a wide number of undefined characteristics that finally chisel one's personality. The ascendant or the rising sign is the sign that was rising over the horizon at the moment of your birth. This is your outward manifestation—what the world perceives about you. The ascendant is also the way you express yourself. Usually one's Sun sign and ascendant are different and the ascendant works as a mask quite often, hiding one's true self, the Sun sign. The ascendant is also quite often revealed in the clothes one wears, car one drives, or any other way one shows one's self to the world. Thus, one who is interested in learning astrology must keep in mind both, the qualities of each Sun sign and the characteristics of each zodiac sign that may rise in a chart at the time of the birth of an individual. That knowledge will certainly enlighten the interested reader to understand a person to a great extent.

But an individual's personality is not totally limited to these two sorts of signs, although they do influence your life to a great extent. What are then the other factors that are important to be kept in mind to assessing one's personality besides the rising sign *(lagna)* and the Sun sign? The simple answer to it would be 'the placement of the planets in the ascendant and the placement of the owner of the ascendant in a chart (*kundali*). Just for example, if the ascendant is placed in the 2nd house, which is the house of hard earned money, speech, family, etc., you can say that the native (whose chart is about to be discussed) will earn money with hard work and will have good family, etc. Further, more in this respect will depend on the nature and the ownership of the ascendant. For example, if Aries is rising in the chart, its owner being Mars, will determine different sorts of benefits and losses to the native according to the sign it occupies in a chart. It will, therefore, depend on the placement of Mars and the zodiac sign it occupies in a house to provide various characteristics and gains or losses to the individual.

Before going further to describe the strength of ascendant, we would like to remind the reader ***that the strength of an ascendant, as of any other house, depends on the nature and ownership of the planet that governs that particular house.*** In view of that we have separately described under the subsection **Transits of the Ascendant in Varied Houses** in this chapter that the placement of the ascendant in a good or less beneficial house will influence the native's career, family happiness, money and property- related gains, and success in life. ***At this juncture we would like to state emphatically that success and failure or any kind of achievement in life, will very much depend on the placement and strength of ascendant in a chart.***

Let us now quickly revise some important matters relating to astrology for that sort of knowledge is absolutely imperative to assess the strength of an ascendant. In this respect we are reproducing two tables that describe planets' ownerships and unfold their exalted and debilitated positions respectively. (Please see **Explore the Power of Astrology**)

TABLE 1
Signs that Planets own

Planets	Signs the Planets Own
Jupiter	Sagittarius & Pisces
Venus	Taurus & Libra
Mercury	Gemini & Virgo
Mars	Aries & Scorpio
Moon	Cancer
Sun	Leo
Saturn	Capricorn & Aquarius
Rahu +	Libra
Ketu +	Gemini

+ Rahu and Ketu are shadow planet and enjoy best in the company of the planets they sit. They give best results when they occupy friendly signs ruled by Saturn, Venus or Mercury.

TABLE 2
Planets' Exalted & Debilitated Positions

Planets	Exalted	Debilitated
Jupiter	Cancer	Capricorn
Venus	Pisces	Virgo
Mercury	Virgo	Pisces
Mars	Capricorn	Cancer
Moon	Taurus	Scorpio
Sun	Aries	Libra
Saturn	Libra	Aries

Besides the above information, we reckon that the reader also needs to know the planets' aspects, which have tremendous impact on individual's personality and way of life. Maharashi Parashar believed that unless one's ascendant has any aspects from the beneficial planets, such as Jupiter, Venus, Mercury and Moon, the native cannot be considered as a good, kind and thoughtful person.

What the Maharishi meant by it was that when the ascendant has aspects from the beneficial planets, their positive effects will always guide him/her to do good things in life. Not only your thinking will be positive, but you will also act for the good of your own family and other people as well. We shall provide examples of this kind when we actually discuss certain horoscopes in this chapter. Let us, therefore, examine the planets' aspects before finally assessing the strength of an ascendant. The following table provides the required information.

TABLE 3

Planets' Aspects from their Positions in a Chart

Jupiter	aspects	**fifth, seventh** and **ninth houses**
Venus	aspects	**seventh house**
Mercury	aspects	**seventh house**
Mars	aspects	**fourth, seventh** and **eighth houses**
Moon	aspects	**seventh house**
Sun	aspects	**seventh house**
Saturn	aspects	**third, seventh** and **tenth houses**
Rahu	aspects	**seventh house**
Ketu	aspects	**seventh house**

General Discussions

Now coming back to our discussion on **the strength of ascendant** we need to understand the nature of **the rising signs** in a chart. We have already narrated certain characteristics relating to the various zodiac signs. But whether these signs bring the same results when occupied by different planets at the ascendant? In this section we would like to explain how the planets rising with their own and different signs at the ascendant bestow benefits or losses to the native by becoming the owner of different houses in a chart. For example, when *Aries is rising* in a chart, the native wants to excel in everything. The native, with a natural force and vigor, tries to perform every task he/she considers important and useful. The native becomes greatly desirous to be successful in life in each task he/she undertakes. The native becomes very assertive and dominating, which may create problems in the family. But if Mars is also sitting at the ascendant in Aries, most of the above qualities and results will surely come true.

When *Scorpio rises,* the native possesses most of the strongest personality traits related to the sign. The native dislikes anybody knowing too much about him/her. When faced with a challenge, the subject knows the self so well that he/she transforms most of his/her qualities to fight the situation. Since the native loves privacy, he/she will extend it to his/her personal relationship too. He/she is possessive, jealous and prone to keep secrecy. He/she does not like to discuss his/her personal problems even with the partner and the nearest ones. It may result in a tendency to cultivate anxiety and harbouring guilt feelings for no important reasons. These characteristics and events will surely take place, if Mars is also sitting at the ascendant.

Likewise, when Libra rises in a chart, it may bestow artistic bent of mind, great insight and taste towards music, cultural activities etc. But if Mars rises in Libra, the results will be different. In that case, Mars owns the 2nd and 7th houses, which, consequently, may bring easy money to the native and cultivate some sort of dramatic characteristics, but the native's personal life will be affected adversely as Mars aspects the 7th house. Likewise, when Capricorn rises at the ascendant, it may provide scientific temper and may incur practical ability in the native. If Saturn also rises in Capricorn at the ascendant, the native will acquire positive qualities and beneficial results will be experienced. If Cancer rises at the ascendant, it may provide highly imaginative qualities and bestow poetic insight and taste. But if Moon is sitting at the ascendant in Cancer, it becomes a very positive force providing the native intensive poetic imagination, extraordinary calmness, serenity, spirituality, long life, cultivation of thoughts implicit with moral fervour, and a beautiful partner who may not live with him/her for a long time.

Thus, when different signs rise at the ascendant, and the planets other than the owner of the ascendant occupy the

ascendant, the native owns the qualities according to the nature of the rising sign, the ownership of the ascendant, and nature of the planet(s) sitting at the ascendant. In fact, we wish to throw light on every aspect relating to the signs rising in the 1st, 5th and the 9th houses and the placement of different planets in these houses. We shall also consider what impact a planet may create on an individual if it owns either 1st, 5th or the 9th house but sits in any of the twelve houses. Let us, therefore, first analyze the transits of different planets rising in different signs at the ascendant. In the subsequent chapters we shall provide explanations regarding the placements of the owners of the ninth and the fifth houses when transiting in other than the 9th and the 5th houses.

Transits of the Sun

The Western astrologers hold that the Sun embodies our true inner self and spiritual path. It represents the ego and the house in which the Sun is placed describes the area of life in which the individual projects these qualities. No matter how the subject appears before others, he/she tends to view oneself from the point of view of the Sun sign that rises in the chart.

When the Sun rises in Aries at the ascendant, it is highly auspicious for it owns the 5th house and sits in the 9th house from there, which, in fact, is the ascendant or the 1st house. The Sun exalts in Aries, therefore, it will cultivate great qualities in the individual's personality. The subject will be daring, honest, straightforward, dashing, highly educated, immensely intelligent, trustworthy, stubborn and quick at taking decisions and will possess excellent memory,. If the fifth house and the ascendant don't have bad aspects, the native will have at least one son who will be highly successful and devoted to the native. At times native's impulsiveness may create some family problems. As the Sun aspects the 7th house, it may create problems to the native's married life. In this respect much will depend on the placement of Saturn in the chart. If Saturn has any sort of impact on the ascendant or the 5th house most of the positive qualities described here above may be mitigated to a considerable extent and the native will thrive with bad temper and unsocial activities. In case the Sun is not afflicted by bad aspects, it is bound to provide the native with honours, he/she may be placed in high positions in the government, may become a very senior officer in military or police setup or even become a very successful surgeon.

When the Sun rises in Scorpio at the ascendant, it will own the 10th house, which again is a very auspicious house. The subject will always be supported by one of the parents in life and will have a senior position in government or private setup. He/she may become a good medical office, a surgeon, a therapist, and a successful scientist. As the Sun aspects the 7th house, it may give an educated partner who will be quite agile in nature but highly emotional and attached with the native. The Sun in Scorpio may bestow haughty temperament, which may affect the native's social and friends' circle. The native may not believe in cultivating an extreme ethical code in life like the one born in Aries. He/she may be in possession of considerably good household and property and may give an attached mother too.

When the Sun transits in Taurus and rises at the ascendant, it bestows artistic qualities, love for music and dance, gains from property, mother, and indicates general prosperity. It provides immense imaginative, poetic and artistic qualities that bring fame to the native. But all such characteristics will be true if the Sun is not afflicted by adverse planets, like Saturn. If Mercury associates with the Sun at the birth, it may give the native a great insight in calculations, mathematics and in general problems relating to life. Such a person may choose to become town-planner, architect, farmer and agriculturist in general. The Sun's aspects on the 7th house will provide a good and emotionally attached partner, who may be sexually agile and possess aggressive temper, will be attached to the native dutifully. It is quite likely that the native may have interest in other women and may hoodwink the partner time to time to save his/her married life.

When the Sun transits in Libra at the ascendant, it is in its debilitated sign. As such, it may create artistic tastes in the native. He/she will love music, dance and painting and will be good at stitching, and many sorts of art- related activities. The native may be a good photographer and a landscape painter. As the Sun aspects the 7th house, the native may not have much happiness with the partner, unless Mars is placed very well in the chart. The Sun in Libra at the ascendant owns the 11th house, which is the house of gains and profits. It is likely that he/she may gain through art- related business and enjoy financial affluence. The native may also be an art teacher. The Sun in Libra may also mitigate the native's confidence, unless it has Jupiter's, or Mars' aspects on the ascendant.

When the Sun transits in Gemini at the ascendant, it brings great expressiveness, agility, quality of taking quick and alternative decisions, displays more flight of imagination than actually possesses. The individual lacks at times power of right sort of discrimination and may not stick to the straight path. At times a Gemini individual may possess strength from good friends and loving brother(s). The native may pursue a lawyer's profession, a mathematics teacher, a clerk, an accountant and a computer operator. It is likely that the native may choose more than one job during life time or change jobs or responsibility within a career. The native tends to do many things at a time to dispel boredom. The disadvantage of Gemini born people is their duel nature as indicated by the sign. It leads to a tendency to be superficial and inability to stick to one task or one person. The subject needs to find positive outlets for all the mental energy he/she possesses to avoid frustration, dissatisfaction and mental tension.

When the Sun transits in Virgo at the ascendant, it can provide a charming personality. But its being the owner of the 12th house would make him/her spendthrift and a loose planner. He/she may possess less insight to see deep into the problems and occasionally choose speech that may turn friends into enemies. As the Sun is in Mercury's sign, it will provide desire to know more in any field the native gets interested. Its aspects on the

7th house may give a good partner provided Jupiter is well-placed in the chart. In general the Sun's placement at the ascendant in Virgo may not be very welcoming, as it tends to mitigate good imagination, bridles capable planning, leads to unwanted expenditure, involves in unfruitful conversation, but may also provide a pleasant and happy going personality endearing to others.

When the Sun transits in Cancer at the ascendant, it owns the 2nd house. The Sun in Cancer may develop emotional and compassionate temperament, may be moody, financially affluent, love research activities, and if Venus is well placed in the chart it could provide jobs and positions in revenue and finance departments, and can make good and loving parents. Such natives are at times highly critical about others, if they don't trim their imagination. Sun's aspects on the 7th house may make relationship with the partner homogeneous until the native is not unnecessarily critical. The native needs to be cautious to have a happy life with the partner as the 7th house belongs to its permanent enemy, Saturn. Much will depend on the placement of the Moon in the chart. If the Moon is placed at the ascendant, or in the 2nd or in the11th house it will bring riches and honours to the native's life. If the Moon is placed in the 12th, or 8th or 6th house, the subject would not enjoy as much financial affluence, neither will be as good temperamentally.

When the Sun transits in Leo at the ascendant, it is one of the most beneficial zodiac signs that may provide a spiritual nature, straightforwardness, always following the truth, unbending attitude and leadership qualities. The native may choose to become a good surgeon, or a professor, or a distinguished army officer or a forest official and possess tidy habits and serenity. Such a subject may be egoistic and possess an aggressive disposition. The native born with a Leo sign at the ascendant with the Sun transiting in it, is often unbending and uncompromising though he/she is full of compassion for the needy and the poor. In case the native gets aggravated on account of unproductive attitude of the fellow workers, he/she is generous enough to forgive them instantly.

When the Sun transits in Sagittarius at the ascendant, it will bestow a very pleasant personality but implicit with ego. Since the Sun owns the 9th house, it is a good placement of the Sun in a chart. It will tend to develop interest in medical field, pharmacy, law or police department. Since a Sagittarius person is freedom lover, he/she may like to take jobs related to freedom of expression, media and would love challenge- oriented positions. A Sagittarius person is daring and may not hesitate to take up work, which may be full of perils. As such, the native would love to be a criminal lawyer, a military officer and jobs of similar kinds. He/she may also choose jobs that involve travel. Sagittarius persons are natural athletes and possess great determination, which will lead them to success. The Sun's aspects on the 7th house from the ascendant may give an educated partner, who would be caring and loving, if the native could bridle his/her ego. If Saturn does not have any adverse aspects on the Sun or if the Sun is not in the company of unfriendly planets like Rahu or Ketu, it is going to help the native to reach good heights in life.

When the Sun transits in Pisces at the ascendant, it owns the 6th house which is the house of ailment, enemies, maternal uncle, litigation, partnership in business etc. As such, it may create ill effects relating to the aforesaid fields. Still the Sun in Pisces may bestow on the individual qualities like kindness, creativity, charitable but clever nature and self-sacrificing demeanour. The symbol of Pisces is two fishes connected by a cord but swimming in opposite directions. As such, a Pisces person likes to work relentlessly in two directions resulting in less success in any of the fields. He/she, therefore, is not able to put entire efforts in the right direction to achieve total success although the native is extremely talented, and spiritually inclined from within. However, the sign Pisces may lead the subject to become a nurse, to take jobs which require human care and welfare, to be a counsellor, a pastoral assistant, an actor or a comedian. The Sun's aspect on the 7th house may give an educated and intelligent partner with whom the native may live sometimes very smoothly and sometimes less efficiently as the native's own nature has a divided perspective.

When the Sun transits in Capricorn at the ascendant, it may provide the native with a practical outlook towards life, self-confident but unbending and ambitious as well. As it owns the 8th house, it may create small health problems from time to time. Its aspects on the 7th house may give quite a loving partner provided the Moon is placed in a beneficial house in the native's chart. However, if the Sun has no aspects from Saturn, the native is bound to get success in life as the zodiac sign Goat suggests. Little by little and with constant efforts the native will rise in life to the desired positions. The Capricorn native is single minded and ambitious about succeeding at anything. And he/she is soon on the way. If such an individual is ever not been able to make it, it is on account of lack of ambition caused by Saturn's aspects on the Sun or any other ill effects. A Capricorn person is often self-made and would do very well when he/she works all alone and not with a partner as often such a person is critical to others.

When the Sun transits in Aquarius at the ascendant, it will own the 7th house in the chart. Unless the Sun does not get Saturn's impact or aspect, the native may have an uneven married life. Without Saturn's influence on the Sun the native may appear cool, glamorous, friendly and always ready with sympathy, advice and practical assistance, still very private in nature. An Aquarian person is mostly positive and personal and sticks to his/her fixed beliefs developed at an early age. But such natives have hard time to letting their true emotions rise to the surface and would not allow any one to come close to them. The native often dislikes a dull job and will soon switch over to another job if he/she feels bored with a particular job. The Aquarian native possesses a natural originality and inventiveness, may have a habitual aptitude for science, scientific research, and can really make his/her way through inventiveness and originality.

Transits of the Moon

The house in which the Moon rises in a chart is the area of life we tend to express our emotional needs and wish to receive and give support to others. Therefore, it is a very reactive and sensitive area of one's birth chart (*kundali*). Traditionally, it is believed that the Moon is concerned to one's heart therefore, it is likely to relate one's inner feelings. It is also believed traditionally that it has to do something with one's mother. Therefore, keeping these two points of views in mind predictions may be made.

When the Moon rises at the ascendant in Aries, it may provide benefits from the mother and may give the native advantages relating to land and property. The native may be involved in construction business and be the owner of quarries and mines. Temperamentally he/she may be slightly on aggressive side and may flare up on trifling matters, but will be straightforward and candid in his/her conduct. If the ascendant Mars is wellplaced in the chart, it may provide the native practicability and make him/her quite affluent property-wise.

If the Moon rises in Scorpio at the ascendant, it may cultivate a biting and jealous disposition that may often affect the native's thinking, which is likely to be often belligerent and not fair to others. Yet overtly it may develop quite an imposing personality which may look quite comely and exciting. As the Moon owns the 9th house in the chart, it will boost up the native's luck by providing him/her good job opportunities, which may vary from medical, police, to business fields. If Mars is well-placed in the chart, it will provide the native extra strength giving him/her a positive and determined direction in thinking that may help the native to decide a proper way to lead life.

If the Moon rises in Taurus at the ascendant, it is a very positive sign as the Moon exalts in this sign. Since it owns the 3rd house, it will give good number of sisters, who will have positive impact on the native's life. If the Moon does not have Saturn's aspects and Venus is well-placed in the chart, it may bestow good luck, friendly outlook, highly imaginative and positive disposition, poetic nature, support from friends and ladies, good education and kind-heartedness. It may give the native opportunities to work in the jobs that are related to navigation or jewellery. In fact, the Moon in Taurus bestows on the native a quality that would provide him good-heartedness, which would always prepare him/her to help others when they are in need.

When the Moon rises in Libra at the ascendant, it owns the 10th house the house of job, profession, ambitions and fulfilment. Traditionally, the 10th house is related to father but according to Western astrology it is related to mother or to one of the parents. In view of that it is bound to provide help from father and mother in shaping the native's life. The native will be artistic in disposition and may follow professions relating to art and craft, love music and related things, likely to be a teacher, may develop uneven relationship with the partner unless Mars is well-placed in the chart. Moon in Libra bestows good education, emotional bent up and quite an introvert personality, unless Venus is well-placed in the chart. It is quite likely that the native may not be a broad-hearted individual, and may suffer from complexes that would not permit him/her to reach good heights in life unless the ascendant itself is highly placed in the chart.

When the Moon rises in Gemini at the ascendant, it owns the 2nd house. It provides good speech and family which cares for the native. The native tends to earn money with hard and honest means. He/she is highly expressive which endears him/her to the people and mates at the work place. The native may produce creative writing material which could be published and bring prominence to him/her. If the Sun, owner of the 3rd house, is well-placed in the chart, it may provide the native with the good company of friends and make him/her very effortful to reach the aims desired. A well-placed Mars will also bring him/her lot of easy financial benefits that will improve the native social status. The Moon's aspect on the 7th house may give him/her a good partner who will be caring but less compromising on the issues that concerns the native most.

When the Moon rises in Virgo at the ascendant, it owns the 11th house, which is the house of gains. It reflects that the native's financial status will be good. The native may get involved in publishing business or may be a writer of repute. Most of such results will be attained, if Mercury is well-placed in the chart. The Moon's aspects on the 7th house may give him/her the company of a good partner who would be cooperative and more adjusting being more enlightened. The native will be highly social and will care for his/her mates as a responsible and dutiful mate.

When the Moon rises in Cancer at the ascendant, it provides great confidence, emotional stability, ethical and pleasant disposition, which is pleasing to the people. If Mars is wellplaced in the native's chart it will help him/her to follow a good profession that may be related to medical, chemical, forest or teaching field. The Moon in Cancer at the ascendant is beneficial to the native in many ways as it not only provides good thinking, courage, responsible and loving nature, helpful to others, pleasant disposition, comely personality, but also brings family's and people's love and respect. But it may create some unpleasantness with the partner who would be often less cooperative and not quite willing to cooperate with the native.

When the Moon sits in Leo at the ascendant, it is quite a sturdy sign that gives him/her a strong nature and single mindedness towards work and people. It also provides him/her a spendthrift way of life on account of Moon's ownership of the 12th house, and a religious disposition that may influence the native's way of thinking to a large extent. It is quite likely that the native may not develop good relationship with the partner, unless the 7th house has good aspects from the beneficial planets like Jupiter or Venus. If the owners of the 5th and 9th houses are well-placed in the chart, the native's life will be smoother and fruitful. But if it has adverse aspects from Saturn, life may not be very comfortable, as he/she would require to fighting hard for most things in life, and will be settled quite late in life.

When the Moon rises in Sagittarius at the ascendant, it owns the 8th house. It may influence the native's emotions and responses at deep sexual level within the partnership and may lead to closer intimacy with each other. The Moon in Sagittarius may help in acquiring wealth and possessions from others.

If Mars is wellplaced in the chart, it may help in providing good technical education. The native may have a philosophic bent of mind and devote lot of time in spiritual and religious activities.

When the Moon, rises in Pisces at the ascendant, it owns 5th house. It is likely to help the native to be creative, social in his/her outlook. The native may be highly imaginative, be a writer, romantic, sports loving and devoted and dear to his/her children. If the Moon is more than 10 degrees in Pisces, it may provide good education and give healthy and decent children who would remain attached and loving to the parents. If Mars is well-placed in the chart in the 1st or 5th house, the native will be very affluent financially and may choose medical profession as a career. If Jupiter aspects the Moon or sits in the 1st house with the Moon, it enhances the status of the native, gives him/her a spiritual insight, enabling him/her to devote most of the time to pursue religious goals. As far as the partner is concerned, the native will enjoy his/her company and feel comfortable at home and outside with the partner.

When the Moon rises in Capricorn at the ascendant, it is bound to give a lot of hard time to the native on account of the partner, though the Moon aspects the 7th house, which is its own sign. The native may be highly emotionally involved with the partner, but the Moon being in Capricorn may not be a healthy sign to the native's life although the native will remain much attached to the partner.

If the Moon bears aspects from Saturn, which is the owner of the ascendant, the native will experience a lot of tide in the married life on account of a self-centred and highly self- styled mate, who may overtly be showy but not truly be what he/she is in reality. It is also going to affect the native's financial status as being over-concern towards the partner may be detrimental to the finances of the native. The native's finances may improve, if Mars is well-placed in the chart but the Moon's association in any form with Saturn may be adverse to the native's peace and happiness although the owner of the 7th sitting in the 1st house is traditionally taken to be *yogakarak* or good.

When the Moon rises in Aquarius at the ascendant, it owns the 6th house, which is the house of litigation, partnership in business, ailment and enemies. The Moon's aspects on the 7th house may not be quite bad, as it is its friend's house. The Moon in Aquarius at the ascendant may make the native highly emotional but most often it may lead him/her to doleful domain as the imagination leads the native to negative thinking creating unfounded fears and doubts in the mind. The native may get involved in some kind of unsocial activities, which may affect his/her social status. Such a placement of the moon may occasionally affect the native's health adversely from time to time unless the ascendant is not well-placed in the chart.

Transits of Mars

All these qualities or weaknesses become the native's second nature, if Mars is placed in the ascendant either in Aries or Scorpio. When *Mars transits in Aries at the ascendant*, it also owns 1st and the 8th houses. Besides, it directly aspects 4th, 7th and the 8th houses. Though Mars is the owner of the 8th house, it being the controller of the 1st, bestows on the native a very strong personality ready to fight every kind of hard situation with an unmitigated strength. At the same time it may bring some kind of problems to his/her married life. Unless the native's partner does not have similar planetary combinations, he/she is bound to experience odd times with the partner. Besides being prone to accidents and physically getting hurt at times, the native will possess unlimited physical strength as Mars being the owner of the 8th is sitting in the 1st house. Mars sitting in the first house also aspects the 4th house, which is related to mother, movable and unmovable property, direction of residence, general happiness, condition of heart, etc. Since Mars' aspect is of debilitated nature on the 4th house, it may mitigate the benefits of that house in general.

When Mars transits in Scorpio and rises at the ascendant, it becomes the owner of the 1st and the 6th houses and aspects 4th, 7th and 8th houses. Mars in Scorpio can bestow a very critical attitude. The native may be prone to some kind of blood disease, may suffer from occasional fever, and kidney disease, at the same time it may lead him to be a good surgeon if he/she chooses to be a doctor. It will depend on the placement and aspects of other planets, especially the owners of the 9th and the 10th houses. Mars' aspects on the 4th house may bring him/her good fortune in respect of property, general happiness and benefits from mother. Krishnamurti Paddati reckons that 4th house is also related to one's education. Therefore, Mars' aspects on the 4th house where the sign Aquarius is rising may bring the native benefits relating to education by providing him/her good educational opportunities. Its aspect on the 7th house may not bring any unusual effects and except for some occasional displeasure from the partner, the subject will pull on with the partner.

Similarly, when Mars transits the ascendant in different zodiac signs, it provides the native with different sorts of benefits as well as mitigates benefits, if it occupies an unfavourable sign. For example, if *Mars is in Taurus at the ascendant*, it becomes the owner of the 12th and 7th houses and aspects the 4th, 7th and 8th houses. Consequently, it makes the native spendthrift, and may direct him/her to live in the north direction (from his original abode). The native may be prone to heart or blood-pressure problems, may affect the mother's health at times, may result in the death of the partner at the age of 31st or 43, may make him outspoken, often leading to skirmishes with others and the partner. It is not a very healthy sign for Mars for it provides the native with less imaginative and intellectual qualities being the owner of the 12th house which is the house of spending, waste and travels as well. When *Mars transits in Libra and rises at the ascendant*, it owns the 2nd and the 7th houses and aspects the 4th, 7th and the 8th houses. Being the owner of the 2nd house it will help the native to earn money from hard work and may bestow him/her with the benefits relating to the partner. Although its aspects on the 7th house may not be considered as good, as it may make him/her marry twice or marry several times after the death (or divorce) of the first partner, yet there is a great possibility that the partner may be helpful to the native in different matters of life being immensely loving, dutiful and kind.

When Mars transits Gemini and Virgo and rises at the ascendant, it owns 6th and 11th, and 3rd and 8th houses respectively. *Mars in Gemini at the ascendant* will provide great financial benefits from the partner, but will keep the native occasionally sick with different blood-related diseases. It will provide the native with a bitter tongue and emotional imbalance. As Mars aspects the 8th house which occupies its exalted sign, it is quite likely that the native may be sports loving, but may undergo operations below abdomen several times during the age ranging from 32 to 43 years. As far as the native's married life is concerned, there is nothing much exciting as Mars' direct aspect on the 7th house is not considered quite beneficial as per the traditions. When *Mars transits in Virgo at the ascendant,* it owns 3rd and the 8th houses. It is likely to benefit the native with a good number of well-placed and loving brothers or and make him/her highly effortful, and provide him/her a less liked but devoted partner. It may not drive him/her to fulfil very hard duties, at times lead to cultivate untruthfulness towards work and partner, and may indulge in some sort of physical ailments relating to loin or near about. Mars in Virgo at the ascendant is likely to produce mixed effects and similarly mixed benefits.

Mars transits in Sagittarius and Pisces at the ascendant will bring occasional benefits, as Mars owns the 12th and the 5th, and the 9th and the 2nd houses respectively. Being the owner of the 5th house when it is in Sagittarius, it is likely to provide the native with at least one or two good sons. It may provide good education, scientific bent of mind but make him/her spendthrift and wasteful in efforts and thinking, as it owns the 12th house also. It may give moderate benefits as far as the 4th and the 7th houses are concerned, but it may bestow certain sort of physical ailment, as it aspects the 8th house, which occupies its debilitated sign, Cancer.

Mars transits in Cancer at the ascendant may be highly beneficial, as it owns the 10th and the 5th houses, which are very beneficial (*kendras*) houses in a chart. The 10th house is related to one's profession, livelihood and the fifth, with education, children, production, romance, publication and intellectual output, etc. Though Mars is debilitated in Cancer, it will bestow favourable influence on the native as it controls two highly beneficial houses, except that it may develop some kind of envy or critical attitude in him/her towards others, especially against those who are more affluent and well-placed in life. Its exalted aspect on the 7th house may also cause early separation from the partner.

When Mars transits in Leo at the ascendant, it is highly favourable, as it owns the 9th and the 4th houses besides it is also sitting in a friendly sign. Its 4th aspect is also highly beneficial, as it is going to give him/her happiness from the mother, provide property-related immense profits may bestow upon him great technical knowledge and benefits from machinery- related industry. Temperamentally, such a person will be straight forward, unbending, to some extent, coarse in his conversation, commanding, possess leadership qualities and will attain life's aims persistently. Such people may lack patience but are highly job- oriented and successful people.

When Mars transits in Capricorn and Aquarius at the ascendant, it bestows great benefits to the native. It exalts in Capricorn and enjoys almost similar status in Aquarius. It works as a torchbearer to the native. When *Mars is in Capricorn at the ascendant*, it owns the 4th and the 11th houses, which are extremely beneficial houses. Such an individual will highly be dashing, possess great impetus for work, contain extraordinary energy, be scientific in temper, become an inventor and possess a charming personality. The native will easily be aroused, harbour jealousy against others, intolerant towards personal criticism, ambitious to excel and reach great heights in life, tall, strong, sports man, easily dejected, less satisfactory family life and less congeniality towards the partner, as its aspect on the 7th house is adverse. Consequently, either the native may remarry or will have extra-marital relationship. As it aspects the 4th house, which is owned by Mars itself, it will bestow great property-related benefits and benefits from the mother. When *Mars is in Aquarius at the ascendant,* it owns 3rd and the 10th houses. Therefore, it will provide great benefits from friends and brothers, bestow great honours from the government and people, the native's name will be heard and known in distant lands, he/she may occupy a high position in police or military setup. But its aspects on the 7th house may bring some kind of permanent ailment to the partner. The native may marry twice on account of disturbed married life or may have extra- marital relationship.

Transits of Mercury

The placement of Mercury in a chart at birth is the area in life in which we need to express ourselves through communication with others, generally in verbal or written form. Mercury also indicates an important sector of our lives relating to pondering involved in our daily lives. The form of communication can be reflected by the sign Mercury occupies at the birth in the chart.

When Mercury rises in Aries at the ascendant, it owns the 3rd and the 6th houses and aspects the 7th house which is owned by Venus. It adds liveliness and wit but makes one slightly aggressive. The subject is often friendly and possesses a number of happy-going brothers. His/her communicating skills are far more than good and he/she may feel at home in the human resource departments where he/she has to deal with a great number of people everyday. The native's area of work may be law, litigation or similar departments where he/she encounters a great number of people everyday. Its aspects on the 7th house are quite beneficial, as the 7th being its friend's house. The partner will be congenial, may possess taste for arts and music and will be cooperative with the native.

When Mercury rises in Scorpio at the ascendant, it owns the 8th and the 11th houses. It will provide financial benefits to the native through writing, through stationary and book-owned shops, through food-related shops, or working as a jeweller, or a goldsmith. It may also give good health and long life, and at the same time quite a thoughtful and devoted partner, who keeps the home welcoming and friendly. The native may have occasional haughty temperament, which may create problems to his social life. Yet Mercury being a planet which has to do with one's thinking, will provide the native a reflective disposition, which may help him/her to provide the opportunity to revise the lost social status.

When Mercury transits in Taurus at the ascendant, it owns the 2nd and the 5th houses, which are very beneficial houses in a chart. As Taurus is a very friendly sign for Mercury, it is bound to provide a honeyed tongue, a highly pleasant disposition and an attractive personality. The native will be highly educated, have even number of sons and daughters, may flourish in publishing or book-shop related business or as an art objects dealer, own shops related to musical instruments or material, may be a civil lawyer, may become a professor, and be a highly cultivated person. Money will come through honest means earned by hard and clean efforts. The native's partner may be a less open-minded person who will be stubborn and a hard-liner, but will be very emotional and sexy. The married life of the native will not be a great success but will also not be a total failure.

When Mercury transits in Libra at the ascendant, it will endow the native with quite a charming personality having artistic tastes, and may make him/her a painter or art dealer, providing great taste for decoration. Mercury will cultivate interest in music and dancing. The subject may become an art or dance teacher, and work in art- related areas. As Mercury owns the 9th and the 12th houses, it will bestow on the native mixed results. As the owner of the 9th house, it will bestow good luck. But as it also owns the 12 house, it will bring some sort of waste in his efforts, plans and indulge him/her in different kinds of activities, which would occasionally lead him/her to spend more than earnings. Such a native will seldom be able to consolidate his/her efforts for greater gains.

When Mercury transits in Gemini and Virgo, it is bound to bring good results and make the native highly communicative both orally and in writing. *When it rises at the ascendant in Gemini,* it certainly cultivates extraordinary communicative qualities and often leads the native to follow lawyer's profession or make him/her a very thriving teacher. The native may be a flourishing publisher, a cloth merchant, own food- related shops or restaurants, and be in possession of great property as it owns the 4th besides the 1st house. Its aspects on the 7th house may not bring the native highly favourable results, but it will also not totally disturb the married life, as one of the partners will be more caring and thoughtful.

When Mercury rises in Virgo at the ascendant, the native possesses a highly charming personality and a honeyed tongue. He/she will be respectful, will command respect from the people, own cloth or books- related business or own restaurants. He/she will be highly communicative both in writing as well as orally. Therefore, the native may also choose jobs related to communication, such as law or teaching or media or telecommunication. But Mercury's aspects on the 7th house may not be quite good and may often bring disharmony with the partner. If the owner of the 7th house, Jupiter, is not well-placed in the native's chart, it may cause disruption (divorce) to the married life. Mercury in Virgo at the ascendant owns the 1st and the 10th houses, which will lead the native to choose jobs or business like publishing, printing, cloth- related tasks, selling garments, or may open schools for the livelihood and family earnings.

When Mercury transits in Cancer at the ascendant, it can make the individual highly emotional, imaginative but less practical. Since Mercury owns the 3rd and the 12th houses, it indicates a few good friends and brothers, but also signifies that the native would need to incur expenditure on the friends and brothers. Mercury in Cancer at the ascendant makes the native feel confident, very effortful, but it also provides him/her a unique way of thinking which is quite original and away from the beaten path or different from the common man's way of thinking. The native may have some sort of writing skills, good at calculations and a taste for poetry. He/she will be of mediocre size in height and may not be very imposing health-wise. Since Mercury also aspects the 7th house from the ascendant, the native's relationship with the partner will be ordinarily good but not quite good. Still both may live happily as the seventh house has aspects from its friendly planet, Mercury.

When Mercury transits in Leo at the ascendant, it makes the native quite determined in his efforts, straightforward, fearless and imaginative. In disposition the native is curt and earns money with good and honest efforts and means. As Mercury owns the 2nd and the 11th houses, its placement at the ascendant is beneficial as far as gains and benefits from the father and job are concerned. Though the native is curt in disposition, he/she is quite effective in communication. As such, he/she commands respect from the people with whom he/she works. Mercury in Leo is in a sign, which is one sign ahead of its exaltation sign (Virgo). It makes the native very ambitious and leads him on to the road to success gradually but quite cautiously.

When Mercury transits in Sagittarius at the ascendant, it owns 7th and the 10th houses, which are very important houses from astrological point of view. Its aspects on the 7th house from the ascendant is beneficial to the native as the sign Gemini is rising there. In view of that it tends to give the native an educated and lovely partner, who, in spite of small storms and disagreements, will stay with the native to boost his/her luck. The native is likely to choose teaching or communication-related jobs and will be liked by people where he/she works. The native will contains scholarly conduct and will like to be involved in acts or jobs that are beneficial to the people. But all such predictions will be true, if Jupiter, the owner of the ascendant, is sitting in a powerful house like the 9th, 5th, 1st or even 11th.

When Mercury rises in Pisces at the ascendant, it may provide the native lofty thinking but most of the time he/she is likely to be involved in a negative or pessimistic sort of thinking, as Mercury is in debilitated sign at the ascendant. Still the native will always like to show overtly positive behavior but sooner or later it may be discovered that others neither love nor respect him/her. But Mercury is Pisces at the ascendant owns the 4th and the 7th houses, which are beneficial houses of the zodiac. There is a great likelihood that the native will have an educated and helpful partner and possess good property, and get advantage from the mother, though at times, she may not be in great harmony with him/her.

When Mercury transits in Capricorn at the ascendant, it provides great luck to the native as it owns the 9th house, but its ownership of the 6th house also makes him/her occasionally sick from cold and cough and other short- term ailments. Mercury in this sign makes the native highly imaginative and bestows on him a great power to solve difficult problems either related to his job of scientific or technical nature. Mercury being in its permanent friend's house in Capricorn bestows on the native certain excellent qualities, such as very polite to the friends, people at work and home, and excellent communicative abilities, which provide him/her some kind of power in the work area. The native is very agile and hard working and ready to deliver goods when entrusted with responsibilities. One more important quality Mercury in Capricorn at the ascendant may bestow on the subject. It is that the native will possess great confidence within and have endless faith in winning the race at the end.

When Mercury transits in Aquarius at the ascendant, it owns the 5th and the 8th houses. As the owner of the 5th it bestows on the native good opportunities to educate oneself and being the owner of the 8th it may give him/her quite a good health with occasional fear of getting emotionally hurt causing dolefulness and withdrawal. Mercury in Aquarius is in a sign, which is just ahead of its debilitated sign, Pisces. As such, it is quite likely that Mercury may generate negative thinking in the native, unless the owner of the ascendant, Saturn, is placed in a good house in a friendly sign. But at times Mercury is likely to give the native lofty ideas, which if directed for good and purposeful life, it may bring good job or business opportunities to the native.

Transits of Jupiter

When Jupiter transits in Aries at the ascendant, it owns 9th and 12 houses. It also aspects the 7th house owned by Venus. In fact, Jupiter's placement at the ascendant is considered to be a highly beneficial placement, as it bestows good imagination, straightforward and right thinking. Its aspects on the 5th and the 9th houses are considered very positive, as they bestow on the native good education, able children, wisdom, philosophy, religion and good luck which affects the human actions from the beginning to the end of life. In fact, it is one's good luck that can make him/her successful in various errands, enterprises, business and activities and make life happier, including having a number of good and able children who are the fruits of a person's life. But Jupiter's aspects on the 7th house from Aries ascendant, is not considered very fruitful. The native's relationship with the partner may not be quite wholesome and though it may not lead to separation, it may not give much happiness unless Venus is very well-placed in the chart.

When Jupiter transits in Scorpio at the ascendant, it is again a very positive sign, as Jupiter owns 2nd and 5th houses from that position. It gives a couple of good sons, good earning from a lucrative job, a commanding voice, convincing and good speech, and happy family. Its aspects on the 5th and the 9th houses give the native good luck, religious insight and beliefs, long journeys mainly for religious purposes and life's earnings. Such a native possesses abundance of physical and mental energy, which are often channelled by the native for highly productive activities. If Mars is wellplaced in the chart, it may make the native a good surgeon, a highly reputed police officer as the native has great physical energy reserves which are combined with mental alertness and good imagination. Its aspects on the 7th house cannot be welcoming, as that house is owned by Venus, Jupiter's permanent enemy. Still if Venus is wellplaced in the chart, it can make the life go with occasional skirmishes with the partner for both are on a different mental wave length that can hardly meet at a point.

When Jupiter transits in Taurus at the ascendant, it owns 8th and 11th houses and it also aspects the 7th house. The native is likely to earn a lot of money though at times the means may not be quite fair. The native tends to invest money and possesses a flair for business. His/her interest in arts and music cannot be ruled out, though it may be limited to liking and being interested into such activities. As Jupiter is the owner of the 8th house, it may give occasional health- related problems. The native may possess a warm sense of humour, be witty and good at winning audience. He/she may also cultivate poetic tastes and compose poetry from time to time depending on the moods. As Jupiter aspects the 7th house, it provides a caring partner, who often commands than to be commanded. The native is generous and loves sumptuous things, especially good food and luxurious living.

When Jupiter transits in Libra at the ascendant, it owns the 3rd and the 6th houses, which are not very even houses for Jupiter. It tends to give a good number of sisters and more women friends who stand with the native from time to time in the need. Because Jupiter owns the 6th house, it may give health-related problems, severe headaches, colds, easily susceptible to cough, head injury and not quite a positive thinking. Since Venus and Jupiter are not friendly with each other, Jupiter at the ascendant may not provide all the positive results, especially relating to productivity and good thinking. It may not give the native quality to analyze matters and problems clearly. But its aspects on the 7th house may bring the company of a good and caring partner who may be bossy but quite accountable to household administration bringing happiness to the family.

When Jupiter transits in Cancer at the ascendant, it brings great influence to the native's intuitive qualities and provides a highly emotionally balanced personality. The native is naturally kind and sympathetic, and possesses great understanding.

The native is caring and protective not only to the family but also to the people in general. He/she works happily for the charitable institutions, and pays a great deal of attention to his/her children. As the native possesses good imagination, he/she is clever enough to broaden knowledge in the fields of work, and becomes highly successful. The native also possesses extraordinary courage and willpower to be successful under any hard circumstances. But as Jupiter owns the 6th house, it is likely to provide some kind of physical ailments from time to time. But it may not affect the native's health adversely. Jupiter also owns the 9th house, which is the house of luck and progress. It would bring help from his/her elders. The native will be highly respected in the society. Since Jupiter aspects the 7th house, it may keep the partner away for a long time or intermittently. Its aspects on the 5th and the 9th are considered very positive and provide good children who may bring luck and prosperity to the family.

When Jupiter transits in Leo at the ascendant, it owns 5th and the 8th houses. It also aspects 5th, 7th and the 9th houses. Jupiter in Leo makes the native highly extrovert, which may be troublesome to others many a time. As the native tends to blow his/her own trumpet most of the time, it becomes a way of life for him/her. Since the native becomes bombastic and showy at times, most people around him/her start drifting away from the native. But such a person has many positive qualities too. He/she is full of optimism, enthusiasm, and generosity, and determined to live fully every moment of life. The native may become an excellent actor or a great leader or a military general, if the Sun, the owner of the ascendant, is also well-placed in the chart. It is also certain that such an individual would possess very promising sons, if Jupiter is not afflicted by any malefic planets like Rahu or Ketu. Jupiter being the owner of the 8th house may bring some kind of physical ailment or small injury in the lower portion of the body. Its aspects on the 9th is absolutely good and, if Mars, the owner of 9^{th,} is also well-placed in the chart, it may bring great luck to the individual through his/her profession. Unless the owner of the 7th house is not placed in the 6th, 8th or 12th houses, the native may lead just a smooth married life though not highly agreeable with the partner.

When Jupiter transits in Sagittarius at the ascendant, it owns the 1st and the 4th houses. It will bestow great property, intelligence, a dashing demeanour, religious and ethical conduct. The native will always love the truth and make it a way of life. Such an individual is optimistic, highly enthusiastic and will cultivate love for knowledge in new fields and areas. He/she would love travelling and will be known as a wise person by the people around him/her. Since Jupiter owns the 4th house, besides property gains, one of the parents will also support the native in life. The native's religious leanings will bestow upon him/her support from the people around and bring good status in the society. Jupiter's aspects on the 5th and the 9th houses will bring him/her good children and good luck in life. If the Sun and Mars are well placed in the chart, the native will experience these results. Such an individual will also enjoy a happy married life, as his/her partner may be well-educated, will be caring and organized in house-hold matters.

When Jupiter transits in Pisces at the ascendant, it owns 10th and the 1st houses and aspects the 5th, 7th and 9th houses. Normally, Jupiter in Pisces at the ascendant makes an individual kindly, sympathetic and caring. Such natives often choose professions as nurses, doctors, social workers, and also priests or philosophers who care for the people's welfare and good. The native tends to be highly emotional, and powerfully imaginative and intuitive. Over caring attitude may bestow on the native worrying mental makeup, which needs to be mitigated. The native is naturally friendly to the people around him/her and that tends to make him/her develop good relationship with anyone the native cares about. It is also quite possible that the native likes the sign Pisces, may be drawn to directions or two missions in life, which may often resist him/her to reach at the top in life. As Jupiter also owns the 10th house, it may bring professional benefits and gains from good jobs. Its aspects on the 5th and 9th will bring good children and good luck to the native. The results of this sort will come true, if the Moon and the Mars are well-placed in the chart. Jupiter's aspects on the 7th house may give the native a caring and educated partner, who is agile, wellorganized, quite thoughtful and loving.

When Jupiter is placed in the sign Capricorn at the ascendant, it owns the 3rd and the 12th houses and aspects the 5th, 7th and the 9th houses. Since Jupiter in Capricorn is in its debilitated sign, it may develop unhealthy and critical imagination and give more number of daughters on whom he/she would need to spend a lot. But such a native will possess a great common sense, caution and attain success through clever thinking and hard work. The native may be pessimistic, an underhand dealer or planner, selfish and determined to reach the goal through fair or foul means though overtly looking very positive. Jupiter's aspects on the 7th will bring a caring, loving and intelligent partner. But the native's own style of reacting and contemplation may cause from time to time some sort of problems with the partner. The native may have a couple of children who may have artistic leaning but not much attached with him/her. If Mercury, the owner of the 9th house, is well-placed it will bring good luck to the native after or around 25th year. In fact, Jupiter in Capricorn at the ascendant is not quite a positive sign. It may give unusual imaginative ability, which will often turn for the good of the self only (make him/her selfish), may develop unethical mental make up, which needs to be curtailed by the individual born in the rising sign of Capricorn, especially when Jupiter is placed in it. In case Saturn is at the ascendant in Capricorn, it will bring an altogether change in the individual's personality making him/her very practical, determined and philanthropic as well.

When Jupiter transits in Aquarius at the ascendant, it owns the 2nd, and 11th houses and aspects usually the 5th, 7th and the 9th houses. It makes the native fairly tolerant, impartial, unsentimental and sympathetic. The native tends to be a great humanitarian and likes to fight for the cause of the suffering and downtrodden. The native has a keen sense of justice and insists that fairness should prevail in every sort of situation. Since both,

2nd and 11th houses deal with earnings, money and gains, it is going to benefit the native in various ways to earn money. Jupiter's aspects on the 7th house may give the native the company of a very devoted partner who will be caring, loving and dutiful. The native will have a number of children who will be well-placed in life. But unless Venus, the owner of luck, is well-placed in the chart, Jupiter may not bring him/her much support from luck. Yet Jupiter in Aquarius may develop literary and musical talents and help to cultivate a scientific and an inventive outlook.

Transits of Venus

If Venus occupies the ascendant at birth, it is bound to create the desire for love, bestow peace, and most attractive personality. The native's appearance is very eye-catching. The subject will be easy-going, loving, and will project harmony by his/her conduct. But these results will fully be realized when Venus rises in its own signs or friendly signs. Let us analyze Venus' transits in different signs at the ascendant.

When Venus transits in Aries at the ascendant, it owns the 2nd and the 7th houses. As such, it is going to provide financial benefits through a good and lucrative job. It may also be beneficial to provide quite a long age and a charming personality, but a sharp tongue. Its aspects on the 7th house may give a beautiful partner but at times marriage may be delayed on account of personal reasons. *When Venus transits in Scorpio at the ascendant*, it owns the 7th and the 12 houses. Though Venus may provide a charming and aggressive demeanour and bring luck through the partner, the native may be curt, spendthrift and wasteful in his efforts and plans. His/her success will mainly depend on the good, thoughtful and devoted partner who will always be standing with the subject in his/her diversity and bad days. But if the owner of the ascendant, Mars, is well-placed in the chart, the native may cultivate a determined and effortful life. It may also mitigate the bad effects of Venus owning the 12th house.

If Venus is in Taurus sign at the ascendant, it will own the 1st and the 6th houses. Being the owner of the 1st it will provide prudence, artistic qualities, compassionate nature, love for music and painting but it may cause occasional illness, as it also owns the 6th house. Its aspect on the 7th may bestow upon him a sensuous nature, uneven relationship with the partner, good luck, jobs in judiciary, or finance department. *When the sign Libra is ring and Venus is placed in it*, it may give the native love for music, sense of decorating home, and make him/her quite talkative. It may give him/her less fair complexion, fear from small accidents, skin diseases, benefits from mother, good education, liking for teaching, couple of sons, and a taste for artistic activities. At the same time as it aspects the 7th house, it may not help developing a very congenial relationship with the partner, though it may not cause a break finally.

If Venus is placed at the ascendant in Gemini, it owns the 5th and the 12 houses and aspects the seventh house. It will provide great insight and intellectual capability, good formal education, and capability to converse with the people and create great impact on them. It will make the native known as a highly learned man and may give more number of daughters. The native will love writing and publishing. He/she may choose lawyer's or teacher's profession or involve in a business relating to bookshop, restaurant or fashion garments. Being the owner of the 12th house, it may also bring some kind of waste to his plans of business, thinking and general efforts. He/she may be spendthrift and waste his earnings. Venus' aspects on the 7th house may help the native to choose a partner at slightly late age but as Sagittarius is rising in that house it will be a marriage of convenience rather than what is really considered welcoming.

If Venus is placed in Cancer at the ascendant, it owns 4th and the 11th houses, which are great beneficial houses in the astrological world. It is bound to take care of home, mother property and will bring wealth from extra income. Its aspect on the seventh house will be quite favourable as Capricorn is rising in that house. The partner may be slightly senior in age and may be dominating, but caring too. Venus' placement at the ascendant as the owner of the 11th house is highly beneficial to the native and it may bring him benefits from the revenue- related departments, may provide him jobs in big firms, industries or revenue department and give him/her good position and status in life.

Venus' placement in Leo at the ascendant may bring money-related jobs like accountants, treasurer, or even cashier. It may make the individual less flexible, hot tempered, talkative, money minded, possess a number of sisters, and provide benefits from the partner who will be caring, if the owner of the 7th house is placed in a good house. But if the owner of the 7th is placed in 6th, 8th or 12 house, marriage will be delayed or the native will choose a partner senior in age and may not be very comely. As Leo is not quite a friendly sign for Venus, the subject is likely to be static, liar, selfish, less imaginative, impolite, showy, quarrelsome, and not quite popular among his family or friends.

When Venus is placed in Sagittarius and Pisces at the ascendant, it owns 6th and 11th houses, as well as 2nd and the 8th houses respectively, besides it aspects the 7th houses too. *Venus in Sagittarius at the ascendant* may develop some sort of knotty thinking and revengeful nature, but being the owner of the 11th house it will certainly bring financial benefits to the native, though not through very clean means because Venus is sitting in its enemy's house. Since Venus also owns the 6th house when it is in Sagittarius at the ascendant, it may get occasional headaches, colds, and similar ailments to the native. The native may indulge in litigation, and create enemies on account of his/her unpleasant disposition and curt speech uttered without much thinking. He/she may often have hard time with his boss, as the job chosen is of less liking, or the native is unable to fulfil what is required of him/her.

When Venus sits in Pisces at the ascendant, it will provide the native with an imposing personality, immense leadership qualities, good speech, excellent memory, creative thinking, problem-solving disposition, cheerful and happy demeanour, and undefeatable courage. He will be loved by women, may occasionally tell lies, but sustain peoples' confidence, possess knowledge of scriptures, and may be a great politician. One of the demerits of such a native is to have extramarital relationships and excessive interest in opposite sex on account of Venus' low aspect on the 7th house. The native will have long life as Venus being the owner of the 8th is sitting at the ascendant. Venus also owns the 3rd house when it is in Pisces at the ascendant. It helps the native to have highly placed brothers and friends always ready to help him/her.

When Venus rises in Capricorn and Aquarius at the ascendant, good results are expected. *When Capricorn is rising at the ascendant and Venus sits in there*, it owns the 10th house which controls professional matters. Venus may provide great job opportunities to the native in financial, revenue and other related fields. The native may have an excellent artistic taste and may be a successful actor and a director of plays and films. Venus in Capricorn at the ascendant also owns the 5th house, which provides the native great educational opportunities, sharpens the memory and enables him/her to be an artist, a writer or a poet of repute. It may give more number of daughters but most of them will be well-placed in life. The native may be a successful play or storywriter.

When Venus rises in Aquarius at the ascendant, it may provide great luck to the native, as it owns the 9th house. Its ownership of the 4th house is likely to provide the native benefits from mother, property, servants, motor vehicles and business related with property and construction. Venus' aspects on the 7th house may not be harmful when it rises in Capricorn but it could be damaging and not quite welcoming when it rises in Aquarius at the ascendant and may bring separation from the partner, delayed or unsuccessful marriage which may give unhappiness. These results may come true, if the owner of the 7th house sits in an unfavourable sign in the chart.

Transits of Saturn

Jupiter indicates individual's intellectual and expensive sides, but Saturn is more concerned with responsibility, rules and regulations that are imperative for an individual to run one's life well. Saturn is concerned with self-discipline and self-respect, one's duties and limitations and also represents the authority figure in individual's life. Saturn is native's ambitious side and is well aware of one's strength and weaknesses.

When Saturn transits in Aries at the ascendant, it owns the 10th and 11th houses and aspects the 3rd, 7th and the 10th houses. Saturn's placement in Aries at the ascendant may make a person confused, full of suspicions, doubts, less active, lazy, showy and less ethical. But on job side Saturn may help the individual to do good especially if he/she chooses a lawyer's profession. The native may do very well as a criminal advocate because he/she is going to use all the dubious means and ways to win. Such a native will have good number of brothers and friends and would earn money by fair or foul means keeping his/her status at stake. The native will have a devoted partner who would abide by him in most of the activities. It is also possible that such a person may wear a mask of religiosity to hoodwink people in order to win respect.

When Saturn transits in Scorpio at the ascendant, it owns the 3rd and the 4th houses, which will bestow upon him/her a good number of brothers and devoted friends as well as make him the owner of movable and immovable property. Its aspects on the 3rd house will make the native highly effortful possessing a great determination to win the race finally. Saturn's aspect on the 7th house gives the native a good and talented partner who would be a good housekeeper, devoted and versatile as well. In fact, Saturn in Scorpio is not always very positive sign as it makes the native dogged in nature, obsessed with sex feelings and overdoing in minting money. The native may possess a kind of short sight, which may not take him/her very far in social arenas. He/she needs to curtail such anti-social activities that would often make him unpopular with his/her friends and people.

When Saturn transits in Taurus at the ascendant, it owns the 9th and the 10th houses. By far it is one of the best placements of Saturn in a chart, as it is in its friendly sign at the ascendant and it owns two of the best houses in the chart. The native will act not only cautiously but also patiently. The native will like to love his/her social surroundings and will make his/her reach goals to attain a remarkable social status. It is quite likely that such an individual may be bit shy in disposition and would not be able to express true feelings openly. It has to be checked, and kind and considerate feelings must be openly expressed before people to show them one's tender heart. Saturn being the owner of the 9th and the 10th will bring good luck through high positions at work. The area of his/her work could be judiciary, acting and directing films, high position in art-related jobs, Company manager, industrialist, municipal chairman, and head of any art college etc. Its aspects on the 7th house may give an aggressive kind of partner who may not compromise much with the native's way of loving, imaginative qualities and nature of work. Therefore, the married life will experience uneven paths—sometimes happy but mostly discontented.

When Saturn transits in Libra at the ascendant, it owns the 4th and the 5th houses. It is an excellent placement for Saturn, as it helps the native to get high education, provides him/her with great movable and unmovable property, and bestows benefits from one of the parents, more likely from the mother. When Saturn is in Libra, the native is very responsible and fair and works well with others. Its aspects on the 5th may provide the native company of educated friends. Saturn may also give the native a dashing partner who is extremely emotional, sexy, and full of vigour to a certain extent but caring too. Saturn's aspects on the 10th may provide him/her vicissitudes in life and changes in job positions are immanent. Such changes are expected after the age of 36 years. In fact, it is a very lucky and progressive sign. Such a placement of Saturn will boost up luck. As the native grows in age, it may provide him/her money, position, prestige, and status in society, but may lead him/her to become arrogant and proud, talkative and spiteful at times, though occasional kindness and tender thoughts cannot be ruled out.

When Saturn transits in Gemini at the ascendant, it owns the 8th and the 9th houses and aspects the 3rd, 7th and the 10th houses. Saturn placed in Gemini tends to develop communicative talents in the native but he/she may be curt at times, which needs to be taken care of. Saturn in Gemini can help individual to develop a great capacity for problem-solving and life-long learning. It provides the individual natural intelligence and gives patience required to succeed in life. As it owns the 8th house, it may indicate some sort of skin disease or small accidents that may not leave any scar. Its aspects on the 5th house may not be very useful and it may lead to loss of brother(s) or uneven relationship with friends and brothers. As Saturn owns the 9th house, it may bring good luck provided Jupiter, the owner of the 10$^{th.}$ is in conjunction or well-placed in the chart.

When Saturn transits in Virgo at the ascendant, it owns the 5th and the 6th houses. Saturn in Virgo makes the individual highly ambitious, responsible and practical. Saturn helps the individual to achieve life's goals, which are more pleasure-oriented. Saturn also tends to make the individual quite methodical and hard taskmaster but an excellent employee. As the owner of the 5th Saturn may give a number of good and well-placed sons but all of them may not be as friendly because it also owns the 6th house, the house of skirmish and enmity too. Saturn being the owner of the 5th house may provide high opportunities of education and learning and give an enlightening insight. As Saturn aspects the 3rd house, it may influence individual's working capacity adversely but its aspects on the 10th may help the subject to get a good job in a communication, media, teaching and even in armed forces, provided Mars is also well-placed in the chart.

*When Saturn transits in Cancer at the ascendant***,** it owns 7th and 8th houses and aspects the 3rd, 7th and the 10th houses. As an owner of the 7th it may give a matured partner who may be slightly older in age than the native and not very fair in complexion. The partner may not be quite willing to abide by the native's desires and like to act according to his/her own inclinations. Such a placement of Saturn may cultivate a worrying personality, a withdrawn kind of person, who may be less overt. Often more pessimistic thoughts may occupy his/her mind. The native will be much concerned with the family and life and devote more time in securing a home for the family and children. As Saturn aspects the 3rd house, it may give understanding brothers and friends who will love to keep the native's company. Its aspects on the 10th house may not be as fruitful and may tend him to change jobs because of less satisfaction and not much liking. Its placement in the 1st house in Cancer cannot be considered to be very healthy and fruitful sign and if the Moon is not well-placed in the chart, it may cause concern and too much worry for the family, kids and friends.

When Saturn transits in Leo at the ascendant, it owns the 6th and 7th houses and aspects the 3rd, 7th, and 10th houses. Saturn in Leo at the ascendant may make the individual an egoist who is proud and strong headed and often dons a serious countenance that may not be liked by many. But the native will possess a real desire to succeed, which would make him/her work very hard. It is quite likely that such an individual may have a caring but less willing and more matured partner with whom the native lives with less affection but more on account of responsibility. Since Saturn also owns the 6th house, it may cultivate unhealthy thought process and blurred imagination that would not often suggest the right ways and means to lead life. In fact, Saturn's placement in Leo at the ascendant cannot be considered a very healthy sign as it is going to lead the native to unethical paths in life making it more miserable, failure and woeful. Much will depend on the placement of the Sun, the owner of the ascendant. If the Sun is placed in a good sign or in a beneficial house and is not afflicted by Saturn, it will surely mitigate the ill effects of Saturn to a considerable extent.

When Saturn is placed in Sagittarius at the ascendant, it owns the 2nd and the 3rd houses. It is also fairly a good placement, as it helps to earn a lot of money and bestows the company of influential persons. It also tends to give a couple of brothers who may not be well adjusted with him/her. Its aspects on the 7th house may give the company of an educated partner who is versatile and good conversationalist, caring and good at house keeping. It is quite possible that such a native may be blessed with an intelligent son, and learns wisdom as he/she grows in age. Such an individual may choose a teaching position, or may work in media or communication-related organizations.

When Saturn transits in Pisces at the ascendant, it owns the11th and the 12th houses. It tends to make the native shy, withdrawn from the public eye, indecisive, but possessing love and abundant sympathy for the people. The native is quite rich in intuitive qualities and spiritually oriented. Such a native is very resourceful and creative as his/her imagination can lead to such activities. But the subject is often over sensitive, which often throws him/her into problems leading to disappointments. Saturn being the owner of the 12th house may cultivate a desire in the native to spend more than what one earns normally. Its aspects on the 3rd house may give him/her good brothers and loving friends. Its aspects on the 7th may also give the company of an educated, caring and loving partner who though not quite agreeable in all matters of life and household, may be adjustable and agreeable on account of the communicative abilities.

When Saturn transits in Capricorn at the ascendant, it owns the 1st and the 2nd houses. It is quite a beneficial placement of Saturn, as it brings money, position and status, and makes the individual very practical, persistent in efforts, resolute in determination, less religion -oriented, immense insight and hard working. The individual is highly disciplined and knows well how to reach the goals in life. Its aspects on the 3rd house may give him/her the company of very choosy friends and brothers but such a native tending to practise privacy, may not indulge much in the company of friends or brothers. Saturn's aspects on the 7th house may not provide the native the company of a very adjustable and responsible partner although the native may stay attached with the partner emotionally.

When Saturn transits in Aquarius at the ascendant, it owns the 1st and the 12th houses. The native born with Saturn in such a sign wants both freedom and order. Being the owner of the 1st house it makes one music lover, sturdy, determined, goal-oriented, spendthrift, involves in unwanted expenditures, very ambitious, critical and jealous of those who excel him/her in status, money and position. Saturn's aspects on the 3rd house may give the native small number of brothers and few friends out of whom only fewer would be dependable and trustworthy. In Aquarius Saturn tends to encourage originality and humanitarian qualities and the individual is highly capable to understand his/her own mind. Such an individual is very candid in expressing opinions may be curt in his/her manner and disposition. As the individual loves independence, he/she prefers to stay aloof and is happy in the company of his/her own. Saturn in Aquarius at the ascendant would normally permit the native to marry late and if the Sun is not well-placed in the chart, it may ruin the married life of the subject.

Transits of Rahu & Ketu

Both Rahu & Ketu are the nodes of the Moon and are known as *chaya grah.* There are various explanations (mostly not quite certain) about their placements and lordships. But as they belong to the group of Saturn and Venus, they must enjoy in a sign owned by either Saturn or Venus or Mercury. Some Indian traditional books state that Rahu gets exalted in Libra or Virgo, but some indicate that except Ketu, which enjoys its position in the signs owned by Mars, Rahu provides most beneficial results when placed in the signs owned by Saturn. Traditions reflect that both these shadowy planets track each sign for nearly one- and-a-half year and provide good or bad results when placed all alone. They retrograde as they move. Therefore, by the virtue of their positions and nature they go backwards to enter a new sign after they complete one and a half year in the previous sign. In view of that our common sense tells us that even if they occupy a beneficial sign or house according to their backward movements (they are placed just opposite to each other at 180 degrees in a chart), they would not give all the expected good results. Basically, they are troublesome and all of malefic nature. For example, if Rahu transits in Libra or Virgo at the ascendant, by far it should give good results but it is certainly going to transmit some kind of mischievous characteristics into the person's nature in whose chart (*kundali*) it sits. We have seen very dashing people with Rahu or Ketu sitting at the ascendant. Overtly the man in whose chart Rahu was sitting at the ascendent, was very popular but when we examined him closely, we discovered that many unethical qualities were incorporated into him. He would tell lies so convincingly that you would take years to discover it.

One more explanation needs to be given about these two shadowy planets. Tradition says that Rahu and Ketu behave or provide results in view of the sign they occupy or the company they keep. That means, if they are conjunct with Saturn, they would act like Saturn and if with Venus, Mars or Jupiter, they would provide results with that effect. They may also provide results befitting to the sign they are sitting in. It has also been observed that both these shadowy planets are considered very powerful in the 3rd, 6th, 11th, and 12th houses. But our view is that even if they are considered powerful in a particular sign or house, they are going to give some sort of malefic, distorted or unpleasant results, as it is their nature and tradition. Therefore, the reader and one who desires to know more about these two shadowy planets, must be open-minded and keep his/her eyes open like a researcher, and try to learn from each new situation in a chart he/she happens to examine.

The Ascendant in Various Houses

We have discussed so far the placements of the owners of the ascendants in different signs at the ascendant only. *Now we would like you to understand the results of the placement of an ascendant in different signs and in different houses.* Before we present discussions on the placement of ascendant in different signs and different houses, we would like the reader to understand what each house of a chart indicates.

Astrologically every house has a meaning and purpose. To understand the houses and the placements of the planets in the houses is one more step to unlock the mystery of an individual whose chart you are going to study. Each of the 12 houses covers a specific area of your life. Any house in a birth chart with more than one planet in it, shows an area of an individual's life that is emphasized and strengthened. But the houses without any planets are active too. It all depends on the ruler of a house and the aspects it has to it. A house without any planet in it could be equally strong as one with the planets. All houses whether empty or with the planets, have houserulers, which describe what is happening in that area of your life. (*Table No.1 & Appendix I*) Thus, the houserulers or landlords are highly important, as they describe what would happen to an individual in a particular area of life. In case one of the planets placed in a house has also its ruler, that house, in fact, has a resident landlord, just like a real landlord. That planet is going to have a great control over what happens in that particular area of life. (4: p.190)

The Houses

The First House

This is the most important house of the horoscope. This is the house of self, the place where the ascendant, personality and self-image resides. It contains the rising sign (*lagna*) and expresses one's personality, temperament, physical health, overall wellbeing, physical characteristics and general attitude towards life. It represents your personal style, mannerism, your likes and dislikes and provides the key to why you look the way you do. It also includes one's early childhood and is closely knitted to your health. If successfully deciphered, the first house shows a sense of control and direction. It is so obvious that the focus of this house is going to be your identity. *When a planet transits the ascendant in its own sign, it will provide benefits according to the nature of the planet rising in a sign. We have already discussed at length the placements of various planets at the ascendant. The reader needs to keep in mind that the planet occupying the ascendant will surely provide benefits to the native in the light of the strength and characteristics it possesses.*

The Second House

The second house reveals one's attitude about possessions, security and partners. It is the house where one will find not only one's money and what one owns, but also what one will own and value, including one's income and those things that one will come to treasure. It also reveals how one feels about one's possessions and will show the best ways how one will earn one's living. It has also to do with one's speech, one's style of conversation, such as, aggressive or polite and family and friendly ties. This house also represents individual's self-esteem, earning abilities and personal resources, making this the house of productivity. Any ruler of ascendant occupying the second house will provide benefits in view of the characteristics the second house contains as well as the nature of the ascendant. For example, if the owner of the ascendant is Venus and it sits in the second house, it will bestow financial benefits on the native associated with art, acting and culture-related activities besides his/her speech will be mild and full of sweet words. *Therefore, the reader needs to remember that the owner of the ascendant when transiting a house other than the ascendant it will bestow qualities, benefits or even losses in view of the characteristics of the house it sits in. It would also possess the qualities the rising sign possesses at the ascendant. Things in this direction will be clearer when the reader goes through our discussions presented with the analysis of the charts.*

The Third House

The third house is concerned with all the nearest relatives, brothers, sisters, friends, cousins, etc, but not parents. This house is additionally concerned with communication, (Gemini) transportation and environment. For example, if one is planning to move, the third house may offer advice about what type of environment (town or country) would be best for the individual. (10: p110) It is also concerned with one's capacities for information gathering and sharing. It includes one's knowledge, short journeys and immediate environment. Traditionally, this house is also concerned with one's efforts towards life's goals.

The Fourth House

The fourth house, in fact, is one's home, the place where a house is a home. In addition of being one's domestic life, it is a place where one can feel to be at home with one's unconscious patterns, habits and emotional underpinnings. It is the house where one's foundations of life are seated. The house is related to one's insecurities or need for emotional security. The natural fourth house is ruled by Cancer. So it is associated with the Moon. Thus, the fourth house is both, one's seclusion and self-protection—the place where one can retreat to and depend on. It also indicates the point of one's beginning. As it is related with the Moon, traditionally it is also related with the native's mother and movable as well as immovable property, happiness received from home, vehicles that one would own and, in general, it is also concerned with one's peace and serenity in life. To some extent, this house also indicates the direction and place or town where one is likely to settle down. This direction can be reckoned from one's place of birth or parental home. Some Western astrologers consider that the fourth house reflects relationships and connections with one's father as well as father's status.

The Fifth House

Traditionally, the fifth house is the house of creativity. Thus, naturally it is related with children, risk-taking, romance and every kind of creative endeavour, such as, writing, publishing, and investments for productivity. One's creativity is not limited to the arts but one could be creative in any field and direction. The sign occupied by this house indicates the nature of one's creativity and self-expression and its ruler indicates how and where one would develop one's abilities to express oneself. The fifth house also has a strong association with pleasure, particularly one's attitude towards love affairs, the act of love (having children) and the ways one translates emotional and spiritual love into physical. Traditionally, Indian astrologers associated this house mainly with children and education, hence with one's productivity and creativity in any form.

The Sixth House

The sixth house is related to the health but not with the physical health like the first house. The sixth house is strongly associated with hygiene and diet, and bowels—all may not be linked to one's physical being. This house also indicates how one handles everyday work and routine whether in business or raising a family. It indicates how disciplined one is when faced with daily routine. This house also reveals (according to the Western tradition) one's attitude towards servants and how one treats those who help in running one's life smoothly. (10: p.111) Indian tradition reveals that this house is associated with litigation, partnership in business, enmity, position and relationship with the maternal uncle, and communicative qualities.

The Seventh House

The seventh house mainly highlights the native's attitudes and feelings about emotional relationships or partnerships. In particular, the seventh house reveals one's deep- rooted needs in the area of love, what sort of partner one looks for and how easy or difficult it would be for the individual to maintain harmony in a partnership. The seventh house should always be interpreted together with the fifth house, which indicates one's attitudes towards the act of love and having children. (10: p.111) Western tradition, like the Indian tradition, also considers this house as the house of partnership and marriage. It is associated naturally with the sign Libra, which is ruled by Venus. It indicates what kind of partner and marriage one will have. But it indicates other kinds of partnership as well, such as, important friends and associates, business partners and legal affairs and agreements. Above all, one's seventh house indicates where one cooperates and shares with others. (4: p.220) Indian tradition indicates that this house has to deal primarily with one's marriage, short journeys and at times vocation as well.

The Eighth House

The eighth house is related with one's shared resources and that includes everything from taxes, insurance and business mergers to inheritances and marrying for money. It is also known as the house of death and regeneration, because it is related to transformation and physical death and deals with transforming physical things into energy. Regeneration is about more than death, too. It's also about individual transformation, whether emotional, physical, mental, or spiritual. It is because of this that this house includes the life forces that are related with sex, birth, and the 'life after life' and death as well. This house also deals with psychic powers, occult mysteries and occult knowledge. (4: p.223-4) It is strongly associated with endowments and big lottery wins. Crime research and investigations are also highlighted with this. Traditionally, (Western) this house is associated with the primal 'life force,' and, as such, it is inevitably related with sex, and with individual's deepest and most fundamental sexual urges, rather than simple lovemaking. (10: p.112) Indian tradition indicates that this house primarily deals with individual's death and at times sudden gains through lottery or inheritance.

The Ninth House

It is one of the most important houses besides the ascendant in a chart (*kundali*) The Western system suggests that the ninth house is everything from higher education to philosophy and religion, from law to long travels and foreign concerns. It also includes politics and all areas of collective thought structures. It is also involved with the development of a social conscience. It is the house of one's social areas, mental exploration, long-distance travels and long journeys overseas, love for seeing new cultures and to know more of the world to gain a new perspective of the world in general. The ninth house is also related to one's efforts in finding new patterns of behavior and how to break or change them, mainly because of conditioning, beliefs, religion and philosophical systems that are behind all of us. If one takes advantage of this house when its owner is well-placed, one can make miracles. It is also the house that is related to publishing and teaching and to convey one's ideas and beliefs openly. As it is naturally associated with the sign Sagittarius, it is the house of exploration and higher mind, mainly of philosophical subjects. (4: p.229) & (10: p.112) Thus, besides the ascendant, the ninth house is another very important house, which describes one's beliefs, liking & leaning and life's philosophies. It is the ruler of ninth house that describes where and in what manner an individual will expend one's mind and develop understanding of life. Indian tradition considers this house as the house of luck and long distance. Overseas journeys as well as every kind of religious and spiritual activity that an individual tends to do is also related with it.

The Tenth House

It is the house that is related to hope, progress and responsibility. It reveals how well one is getting on in the world—not only financially but also in terms of fulfilling one's deepest aspirations, dealing with responsibility and authority, traditional values and social status. It is the house, which indicates about one's profession and substantial increase in one's social status. It is the house of one's reputation and career. It is the house where one can find everything outside the home—community standing, social role and what others think of about the individual. Some consider this as the house of ambition, aspiration, and attainment. This house is also related to one of the dominant parents—preferably father. It is the house, which indicates success through one's own efforts and a reflection of one's image and achievements. According to the Indian traditions, the tenth house is related to one's *karma* (actions) and profession. It is also the house that reflects the native's father's profession and social status. The sign that rises in this house indicates the subject's profession, life's achievements and also the amount of leaning towards religious activities.

The Eleventh House

Western astrologers reckon that the eleventh house reveals how one is related to other people socially and is much concerned with friendship and society. This house strongly emphasizes how the native would like to engage with the world. It reveals native's attitude towards political and social opposition and intolerance. It also indicates how much time the native would give to charitable and humanitarian causes and how he/she works with others, especially in large groups. It also indicates 'whether the individual would possess genuine affinity for public office!' Indian traditions identify this house with the native's personal income, gains through relatives, parents, sudden gains through unknown and undisclosed means, gains through excellent business, general affluence and prosperity. In fact, it is the house, which indicates how much wealthy the native should be in his life and how much social status he/she will gather through the riches. A well-placed owner of the eleventh house in a chart indicates that the native will surely lead a wealthy and prosperous life.

The Twelfth House

Western astrologers reckon that this house indicates escapism and isolation. It is also related to hospitals, prisons and mental institutions and all such places where one is likely to experience loneliness and seclusion. It is the house of mystery and related to most psychological problems of the native. (10: p.113) Sometimes this house is also called as the house of sorrows, secrets and self-undoing and it is certainly the most mystical house. It is the house where one finds one's subconscious and the unknown after all. Some Western astrologers reckon this house as the house of troubles, but also make it clear that one's consciousness resides there. This house can lead to self-transcendence, moving one beyond the ego and to what is there beyond the self. (4: p.243) Indian tradition reckons that this house indicates waste, expenses, losses, long and short journeys and *moksha* as well. In fact, if the owner of this house occupies any beneficial sign or is conjunct with a beneficial planet, it is certainly going to mitigate the good effects of that house. More things about it will be discussed when we provide examples of that nature.

Discussions on the Transits of Ascendant

Before we come to the actual discussion on the transits of ascendant in different houses with the help of actual examples, let us discover certain rules, which would enlighten us clearly on this issue. But the reader must keep in mind the characteristics attributed to each house before coming to any conclusions. ***The ascendant will provide results in view of its placement in a particular house and bestow benefits or losses to the native, if it occupies a friendly, exalted, beneficial or a malefic sign respectively.*** For example, if the ascendant is placed in the 5th house, which occupies a friendly sign, it will make the native creative and surely give a number of good sons whose position and status would be great in the public and, consequently, boost up the native's status too.

It may bring romance in the individual's life and may influence his/her married life. ***Thus, according to the placement and the nature of an ascendant in a particular house and in a particular sign, good and bad results will be experienced by the native during his/her life time.*** Actual examples of that kind will be provided hereunder for the benefit of the reader when charts (*kundalies*) will be analyzed. Let us, therefore, consider certain rules that would help in understanding the effects of the placements of ascendants in different signs and different houses in charts. The reader is implored to keep the following rules in mind before and after a chart is put to analysis.

The Rules

1. *The owner of the first house being absolutely important and powerful, must bestow highly beneficial results in its own sign or in a friendly or an exalted sign when placed in the 1st, 2nd, 4th, 5th, 9th, 10th or 11th houses irrespective of its ownership of the other sign rising in a different or a less beneficial house.*
2. *The ascendant becomes especially strong and elevates the native's status when it aspects 9th or 10 houses or aspects the owners of these houses transiting in 9th or 10th houses. In that case it provides great luck, social status and financial affluence, peace and happiness from family & friends.*
3. *The ascendant bestows results in view of its placement in a house. Thus, if the ascendant sits in the 4th house it will bestow property and vehicle related-benefits, and happiness and support from the mother; if it sits in the 5th house it will provide good education and bless the native with good and able children; if it sits in the 11th house it will give money-related advantages and boost up social status of the native; if it sits in the 7th house it may give a loving partner to whom the native will be very caring.*
4. *Likewise if the ascendant sits in the 6th house, it may give some sort of illness, litigation, trouble with the business partners and unaccounted losses created by enemies except that if it sits with a powerful or exalted planet which may not be its natural enemy (then it would not yield bad results); if it sits in the 8th house it may create excessive sex drives especially when Mars is in the ascendant and gives the native some kind of 'life force' that would bring him/her great*

progress, success and achievement; if it is in the 3rd house, it may make the native highly effortful, creative, friendly and social.

Example 1

Given below is the chart of a native who has been a DEO in Education in a State Education set up.

Native born on 21st December, 1938

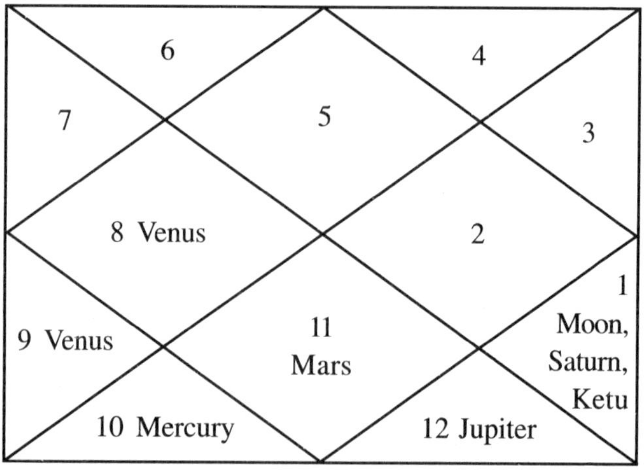

Discussions

The native's ascendant is Leo and its owner, the Sun, is placed in the 5th house. The owner of the 5^{th,} Jupiter, is placed in the 8th house in its own sign. The 5th house naturally belongs to the Sun. As such, the Sun's placement in the 5th house is highly beneficial and has provided great benefits to the native, blessing him with three highly educated sons. Out of three, two are wellplaced as senior officers in the Revenue Department in the Central Government. The third son is a teacher whose placement and earnings cannot be categorized as ordinary in the present circumstances. The owner of the 5th house, Jupiter, is placed in the 8th house, the house of life force and energy. It has bestowed altogether good effects on the native's productivity, that is, educational output. The native possesses a postgraduate degree and a Ph.D. in Education. He retired a few years ago as a District Education Officer from the State government services. The aspects of the owner of the ninth, Mars, on the ascendant has accelerated the strength of the ascendant providing the subject energy and determination to work for progress.

Example 2

Given below is a Senior Surgeon's chart showing the placement of the ascendant in the 11th house.

Native born on 27th May, 1950

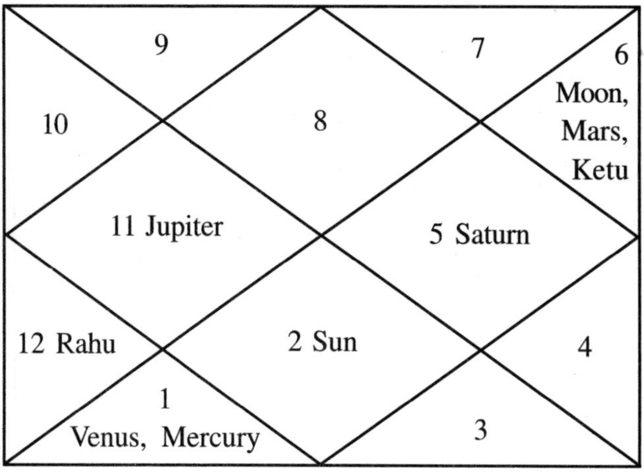

Discussions

The owner of the ascendant is placed in the 11th house, the house of gains and social status. As such, the native is wellplaced in life, financially and socially affluent, possesses a good house, quite an expensive car along with other amenities. He has been enjoying the position of a senior medical officer, as in charge of a Government hospital in the State Government. His wife held a senior teaching position in a Government Medical College in the same State and town where her husband has been employed. She died a few years ago but she left her pension for her daughter (mitigating financial burden of husband) who is still studying. Besides, the ascendant's aspects on the 5th, has benefited the native with two capable engineer sons who are in America and have been helping the native financially time to time.

Example 3

Given below is a suitable chart of a Professor of Chemistry showing the ascendant's placement in the 11th house.

Native Born on 21st March, 1953

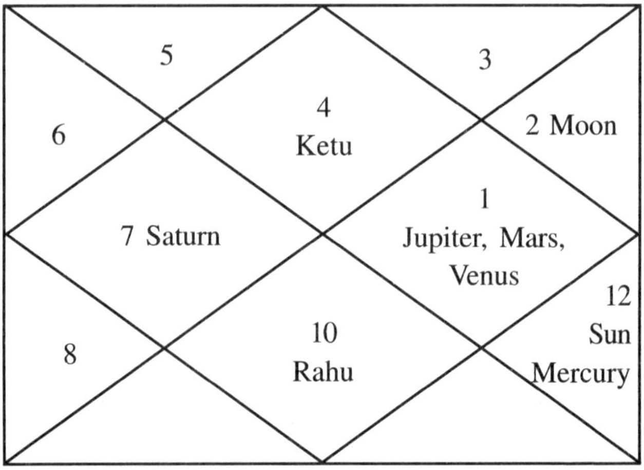

Discussions

The owner of the ascendant, Moon, is placed in the 11th house in an exalted sign, as such, it indicates gains and financial affluence. The 11th house is also related with social status and popularity. The native is quite affluent financially and enjoys good popularity among his colleagues and the people. He is wellplaced in an established University and popular among his students and staff. The Moon's aspects on the 5th house though of debilitated nature and Mars's aspects on the same house has blessed him with a daughter and two sons, who are doing good education-wise. Ascendant's aspect on the fifth house, which is its friend's house, has provided creativity and insight in the native. As such, the subject has produced successfully a number of Ph.D. scholars and published some books and articles in his own field and the field of astrology as well.

Thus, good placement of the owner of the ascendant has provided the native with financial betterment, social status, and professional productivity.

Example 4

Given below is an excellent example of a very senior and successful High Court Advocate's chart showing the placement of the ascendant in the 9th house.

Native Born on 26th April, 1945

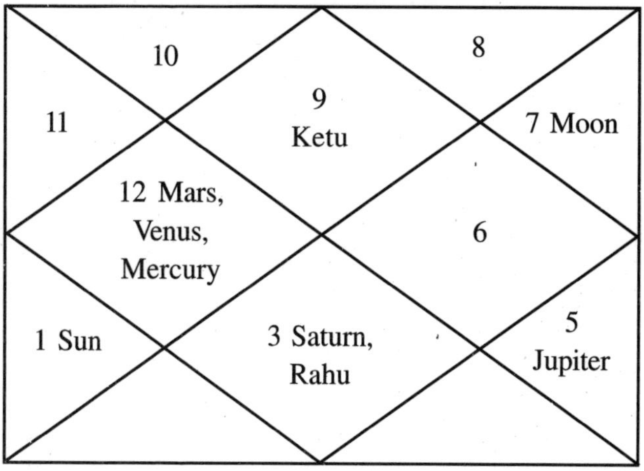

Discussions

It is one of the best examples of ascendant's placement in a chart. Jupiter, as an ascendant, is very powerful and well-placed in Leo in the 9th house which is Jupiter's natural friend's house. The Sun, owner of the 9th house, is sitting in the 5th house in its exalted sign. Jupiter's aspects on both, the ascendant (which is its own house) and the Sun, the owner of the 9th house, has provided immense power to the ascendant. Consequently, colossal affluence and status has been bestowed upon the native.

It has provided him with great luck, financial and social affluence, great status in public, a good mansion, expensive cars and excellent public connections including two very capable and highly educated sons. As a criminal lawyer the native has a roaring practice and has been enjoying great reputation in the high court. If Saturn had not extended its aspects on the ascendant and the owner of the ascendant, the native would have not chosen criminal side for practice.

Example 5

Given below is the chart of a very senior IAS officer serving in the Indian Administrative Services.

Native born on 19th February, 1961

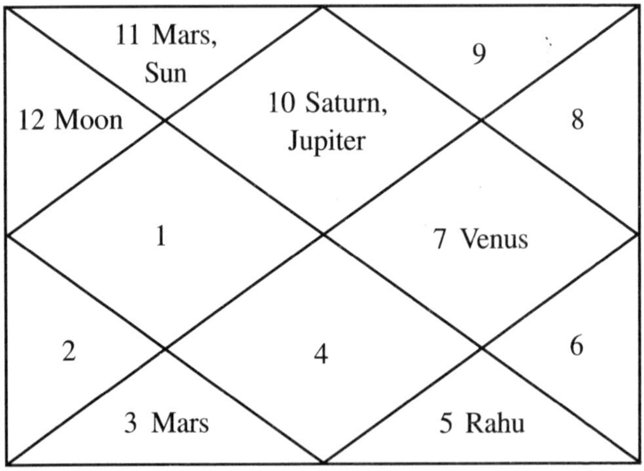

Discussions

Native's ascendant, Saturn, is transiting in its own house at the ascendant. Jupiter is also sitting there in its debilitated sign making *chandal yoga,* which is not quite a beneficial combination as it generates amoral disposition. But the owner of the ascendant and the owner of the 10th house have some kind of ties with each other. Not only that Venus is Saturn's best friend, but Saturn exalts in Libra also. Hence, ascendant's aspects on Venus in Libra, has accelerated the beneficial effects of the 10th house providing the native the position of an IAS officer. The native started his career as a Lecturer, became an IPS but later on appeared at the IAS examination and stood 8th in merit and was appointed as an IAS officer. Both the ascendant and the owner of the 10th Venus are responsible to offer the native such sort of job opportunity but primary role is that of Saturn, which is the owner of the ascendant. Thus, ascendant when aspects the 9th or 10th, it provides the native with great job opportunities, financial affluence and social status.

Example 6

Given below is a suitable example of an Indian Air Force Group Captain's chart showing the placement of the ascendant in the 8th house.

Native born on 26th April, 1924

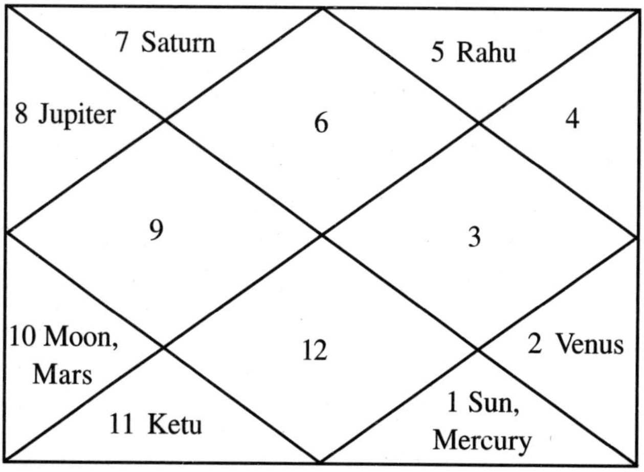

Discussions

This is a chart of a native who was a group Captain in the Indian Air Force and was honoured by two Veer *Chakras* and a President Medal. He also fought in the World War II and was awarded Victoria Cross, the highest gallantry award during the British period for courage. His ascendant is placed in the 8th house and is conjunct with the exalted Sun. A conjunct is usually considered as an aspect. The 8th house is associated with 'life force', regeneration, and transformation of emotional, spiritual or physical forces to utility. As such, the native put all his energies into a vital physical force transforming that to a great life force, and took every opportunity to win all those honours in his own lifetime.

As Mercury, which is considered a light- footed god in Greek legends, is quick, alert, and is the embodiment of wisdom, it was induced courage being in conjunct with the exalted Sun giving the native an extraordinary fortitude and immense winning qualities. As a person he was a fine man, who cared for his family, people and country and led a very upright life implicit with honesty, quick disposal and rational activities, aggravated at times but soon calmed down. The Group Captain died around three and a half years ago but he will always be remembered for his great deeds for the country.

Example 7

Given below is the chart of an Indian Cricket Wizard whose ascendant is sitting in the 7th house. He is still very active in the Indian Cricket and has earned many world records for himself and his country.

Native born on 24th April, 1973

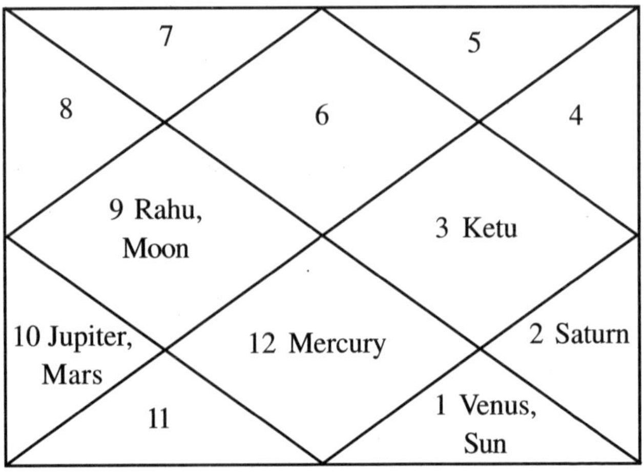

Discussions

The above chart belongs to an Indian cricket wizard, who has earned a great name for himself and for his country and is ranked after Sir Bradman, the Australian batsman. It's an example of an ascendant placed in the 7th house in its debilitated sign.

The debilitated owner of the ascendant, Mercury, has its exalted aspect on the ascendant It has restored all the benefits to the native irrespective of its placement in the debilitated (*neech*) sign. There are other factors, too, to give the cricketer early success and great name and fame. Exalted Mars has its aspects on the exalted Sun and Jupiter aspects Saturn sitting in the 9th house (house of luck) the owner of the 5th house, the house of creativity. Though Mercury is in its debilitated sign, it makes *neech bhagna yoga*, means Mercury's sitting in the debilitated sign does not affect the native adversely. On the contrary, it supports him by its exalted aspects, providing him, agility, courage, intelligence, fame and good footwork.

Example 8

Given below is the chart of a successful Dental Doctor whose ascendant is placed in the debilitated sign in the 10th house

Native born on 2nd March, 1966

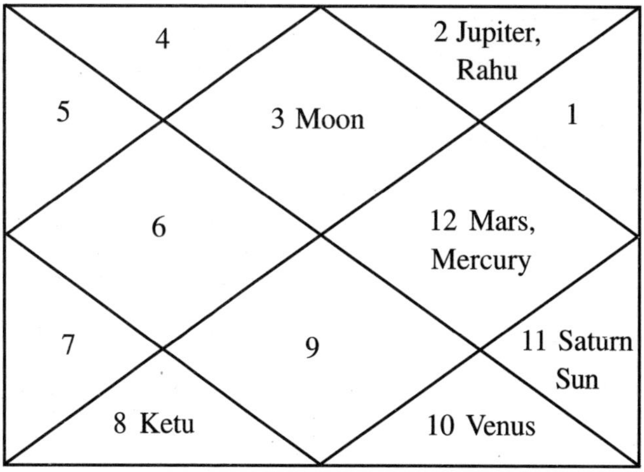

Discussions

The above chart belongs to a lady dental doctor employed in a State government hospital. Debilitated ascendant, Mercury, is placed in the 10th from the ascendant with Mars. Mars aspects the ascendant (Mercury) from the 10th and provides strength to the ascendant, Mercury, being conjunct with it. Mars is always considered beneficial when placed in the 10th house, more so when it owns the 11th house, the house of gains and social status. Consequently, Mercury has provided the native a good and a very lucrative job in a government institution. Besides her basic job, she also visits a couple of private dental colleges in other States to deliver lectures and hold practicals for the dental college students. This brings her additional income, which is highly lucrative and gainful. The native not only possesses a great mansion, but also has an expensive car and at an early age she is highly affluent in all respects. Thus, an ascendant which may be debilitated, but if it sits in the 10th house from its own position (ascendant), it becomes (*yogkarak*) highly beneficial.

Example 9

Given below is the chart of a retired Major General in Indian Army, whose ascendant is placed in the 5th house.

Native born on 6th November, 1941

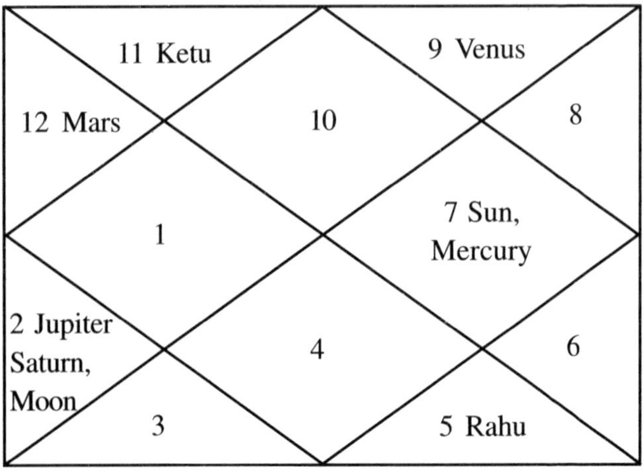

Discussions

The above chart belongs to a native who retired from military service as Major General a few years back after obtaining *Param Veer Chakara*, the highest medal for gallantry. Though he acquired high positions in military service on account of the Sun's placement in the 10th house and Mars aspect on it from the third house, the position of the ascendant is also highly beneficial. Saturn as ascendant, transiting in its friendly sign Taurus, is sitting with the Moon, the owner of the 7th house which is also a kind of *rajya yoga*. It is bound to give honours, social status, money, educational attainment and ability to solve problems. The owner of the 9th Mercury is transiting in the 10th with the Sun, providing the native good luck, intelligence and reflective capability. The ascendant Saturn's placement in the 9th in its natural friend's sign makes the native highly productive and full of wisdom. The native is not only pragmatic but also highly capable to take actions after giving careful considerations and follow through. These are high achievements of the ascendant.

Example 10

Given below is the chart of a retired Professor of Philosophy whose ascendant is placed along with the ruler of the ninth in the 3rd house.

Native born on 1st January, 1933

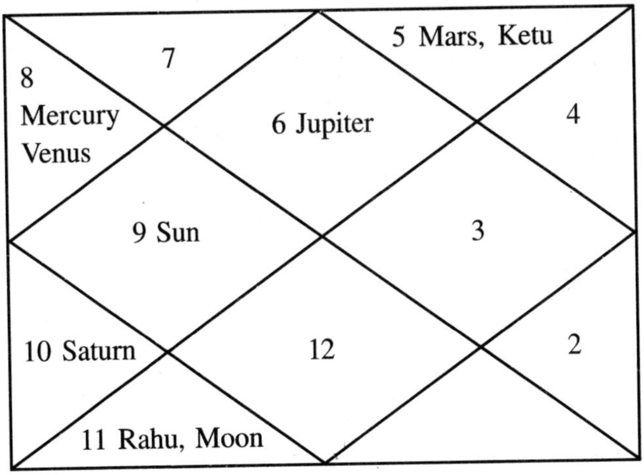

Discussions

The ascendant Mercury, placed in the 3rd house along with its natural friend, Venus, helped the native to acquire gradually everything in life as by the virtue of the ascendant's placement in the 3rd house, it made him work hard, highly effortful and productive. Besides, the owners of the 9th and 10th (Venus & Mercury) are conjunct in the 3rd house, they also have aspects on the 9th house which is the house of luck, higher education, social status and affluence. Mercury being the owner of the ascendant, along with Venus provided the native taste for writing and bestowed on him great capability of publishing books and articles. The native retired as a Professor of Educational Philosophy from an established Institute of Higher Learning affiliated to a University around twelve years back. He has been constantly busy in publishing and in academic activities even after twelve years of retirement and has been visiting Europe & America since last 34 years. Thus, when the ascendant is conjunct with the owner of the 9th or 10, it forms *rajya yoga.* But if this conjunction aspects the 9th house, it provides great luck to the native, giving affluence, social dignity, higher learning, foreign travels, happiness and positive productivity that is beneficial to the community.

The above referred 10 charts (*kundalis*) contain the analysis of the placements of different kinds of ascendants transiting in varied houses. If the reader keeps in mind the aforesaid rules, it would be easy for him/her to understand how different ascendants placed in the 1st, 4th, 5th, 7th, 9th, 10th and 11th houses work positively and bring great luck and beneficial results. Except analyzing the placement of ascendant in the 12th house, we have examined the ascendant's placements in the 1st, 3rd, 4th, 5th, 7th, 8th, 9th, 10th and 11th houses. We have also discussed briefly its placements in the 6th, 3rd and 8th houses. The following examples provide analysis and results of ascendant's placements in the 12th house. Let us first go with the rules, which will help us understand its nature and behavior when placed in the 12th house.

Rule 5. When the ascendant is placed in the 12th house, it may bestow upon the native a strange mental makeup

giving him/her a spendthrift nature, highly critical towards others and frequently conceiving improper plans. The Native may be a schemer, constantly doubting one's own capability, possessing over ambitious assessment of the self, always expecting others to do more for him/her, unforgiving, easily hurt, emotional and impulsive. The native's impulsive behavior may indulge him/her with unnecessary skirmishes and give him a reputation of a quarrelsome and a cunning person, but ultimately he/she may be redeemed on account of his/her quality of analyzing matters with depth and great attention. Therefore, placement of the ascendant in the 12th house should not altogether be taken to be bad for it has some silver lining too. At the same time if the owners of the $9^{th,}$ 10th or 11th houses are well-placed in the chart, the ascendant placed in the 12th house may not affect the native so adversely. As far as financial affluence and other benefits are concerned, the owners of the 9th, 10th, 11th or the 4th houses may take care of it. Let us examine a couple of charts to clarify our point of view.

Example 11

Given below is the chart of a successful Pathologist whose ascendant is in the 12th house.

Native born on 10th January, 1959

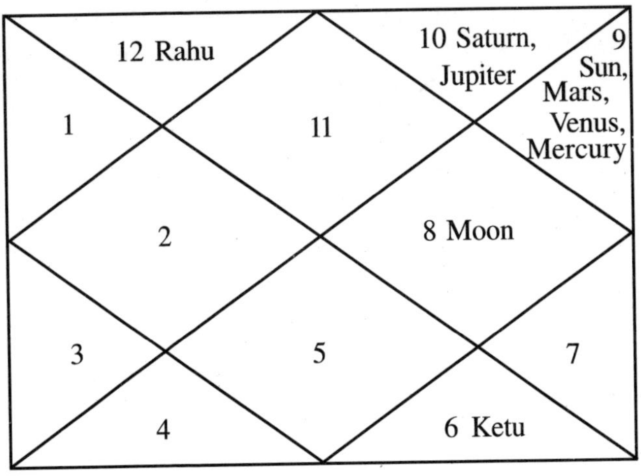

Discussions

The above chart belongs to a doctor who is MD and busy in private practice, earning quite comfortably having fairly good reputation as a pathologist. His ascendant, Saturn is placed in the 12th house, which often becomes the source of dissatisfaction and is polluting the native's imagination. Although he possesses property worth more than hundred thousand dollars, he is often dissatisfied and his desire to get more is seldom mitigated. Traditionally, Saturn is not considered altogether unbeneficial in the 12th house, yet it may cause constantly unhealthy thinking, irrupting dissatisfaction and a feeling of inadequate fulfilment. However, the sign Aquarius represents persistent development of the intellect through communication. People born with this rising sign do anything to avoid their boredom, care little for what others think of them, especially when they have determined their own particular cause. They also possess an ambition, which is always for humankind rather than simply for their own-self. People with Aquarius ascendant have a unique ability to connect to the masses through unusual forms of communication. (4: p.49)

The doctor possesses most of these qualities and he is also quite an affectionate communicator. Besides, the placement of the owners of the 4th, 9th (Venus), 5th and the 7th in the 11th house, has benefited the native with colossal property, good education and gains through the partner (wife). But the ascendant, transiting in the 12th house, may certainly be the cause of dissatisfaction to the native keeping him often on his toes for no serious reasons.

Before summing up our discussions on the strength of the ascendant, we would like to reflect a few more things to ascertain the ascendant's strength in a chart. We have already discussed that ascendant's placement in the 1st, 4th, 5th, 7th, (even in the 3rd and 8th), 9th, 10th and 11th houses is highly beneficial. It is also extremely beneficial when the ascendant is conjunct with any of the above referred beneficial planets or if it exchanges its positions with any of these, or if the ascendant (rising sign) as well as its owner have aspects from the friendly and beneficial planets. But there are some other placements of an ascendant that may make it extremely weak and unfulfilling. Let us first illustrate the rule.

Rule 6. If both the ascendant and the rising sign have aspects from the unfriendly planets or if they exchange their signs with their enemies, it is bound to bestow bad results.

Please refer back to our ***example No.11*** given above and verify the above statement. Saturn's debilitated aspects on the ascendant, has affected the native's disposition and thinking adversely. ***That leads to state that when planets like Saturn, Mars, or the Moon's nodes Rahu and Ketu exert their debilitated aspects on the ascendant, they may bring bad luck, failure, dissatisfaction, disappointments and less affluence. So is the case when the ascendant and its enemy-planet exchange signs (houses) with each other. We produce one more chart (kundali) for the benefit of the reader to confirm how ascendant and its enemy when exchange positions with each other, affect the native very adversely.***

Example 12

Given below is a native's chart in which the ascendant and its natural enemy have exchanged their positions.

Native born on 5th February, 1979

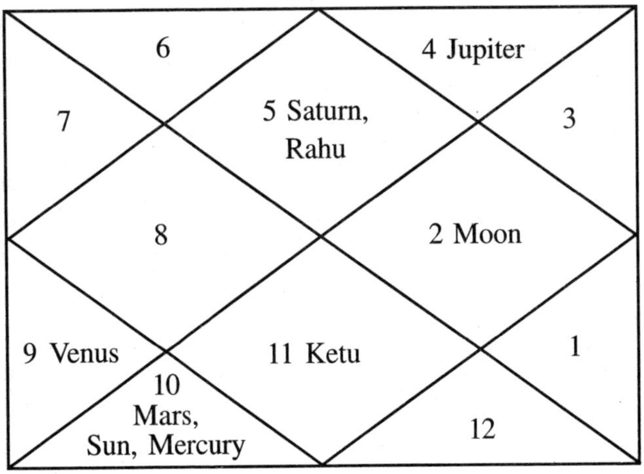

Discussions

The ascendant Sun is placed in the 6th house and the owner of the 6th house Saturn is placed at the ascendant. Perhaps it is one of the worst examples of a conjunct (aspect) of two planets, which has totally corrupted the native's mind, making him alcoholic at a tender age. It is disheartening that just at an early age the native started drinking and is unable to relinquish that habit even after he has reached almost 27 years. Both the parents are highly educated, possess clean and good disposition worthy of following by others. The native possesses a postgraduate degree in Political Science and has been planning to submit his Ph. D. thesis when we are analyzing his chart. In fact, his alcoholic habit is not letting him fulfil what he desires to attain in life, although he is quite capable to achieve a good position in life, if he were free from that ill habit. The 6th house is the house of illness and indisposition. Therefore, its owner sitting at the ascendant has turned tables against him by not letting him possess the strength of willpower and determination that would have checked the temptation of drinking.

Well, there could be more combinations and aspects from the good or malefic planets that would affect the ascendant's strength either favourably or adversely than what we have given in this chapter. But if the reader keeps in mind **The Rules** given here above, and keeps in view what we have discussed under the subheadings, like **The Ascendant in Various Houses,** including Discussions on **Transits of Ascendants,** it would hopefully enlighten him/her in determining the ascendant's strength. It would also help in evaluating a chart quite successfully. Considering that quite enough has been discussed about the Ascendant or the Rising Sign, we proceed to discuss next **the 9th house,** which we reckon equally important and should be considered next to the ascendant.

✡ CHAPTER THREE ✡

The Ninth House

House of Luck, Foreign Travel & Higher Education

Everything in one's life happens in one of the houses. When we look at a chart, the first house represents one's physical self, personality, attitudes, lifeforce, willpower and likes and dislikes. Likewise, the ninth house represents social areas of higher education, philosophy, religion, law- abiding qualities and travels. Traditionally, it is also known as the house of luck, religion, one's beliefs and overseas travels.

The natural owner of this house is Jupiter and the sign that rules it is Sagittarius. This is the house, which discloses clues to one's philosophical viewpoints. It provides one's leanings towards religion and spirituality. This house provides an idea of the native's ongoing education and long distance travels that he/she might plan and undertake in life. One can plan and take advice after observing the placement of the ninth house, whether one should think about taking a year off to explore the world. This house is traditionally (Western) consulted when someone is planning to live or study abroad, work in the travel or export industry, pursue a career in teaching, mainly at the university level. Law, publishing, language skills, literature, positions in temples or shrines, inspirational literature, preaching, medicine and army career are some of the concerns of the ninth house. (10: p.112)

Features Accredited

The 9th house naturally belongs to Sagittarius. As such, a Sagittarius person should possess the qualities that are accredited to the sign Sagittarius. In zodiac tradition a Sagittarius is warm, idealistic, impulsive and fond of spending extravagantly as well as sharing of ideas. A Sagittarius person often wastes his earnings rather than to invest them in real estate or any such purposes. At home in any climate the archetype (Sagittarius person) loves travel, new activities and sporting competition. The cultivated archetype prefers frequent changes in his home settings. A Sagittarius is a thoughtful forward-looking type who loves to accomplish different tasks by envisioning the whole picture. The archetype applies vital ideas to problem solving. The type's enthusiasm inspires others into projects. Because of that a Sagittarius traditionally succeeds in exploration, teaching, medicine, theatre and team-sports. Such a person is good at languages and loves to involve in discussions and debates concerning literature, religion and philosophy. This kind of person readily makes friends and welcomes activities requiring skills, energy and firm aim. (12: p.175)

When a Sagittarius is an adult, he does not like desk jobs and prefers to work in the open air. He likes to be a soldier, pilot, geologist and animal trainer. He supposedly rises to the position of authority. Good examples of Sagittarius are Atal Behari Vajpai, J. F. Kennedy, Abraham Lincoln and Winston Churchill. Both Lincoln and Churchill led their nations to win for the right cause, they had in their mind. Lincoln had a vision. He said, "As I wouldn't be a slave, so I wouldn't be a master. This expresses my idea of democracy." Thus, Sagittarius people are visionaries and with their complete vigour fulfil their dreams. (12: p.176) Likewise, Vajpai and Kennedy also had visions, which they tried to fulfill in their best possible ways.

Typically a Sagittarius would change jobs frequently, seeking impulsively new fields for work and new areas or communities where the type is more sympathetic, wilful and creative. Such a person will possess self-direction, but choose amusement over intense work sessions. In matters of morality and ethics this type may tend towards fanaticism but in business the Sagittarius would press for excellence. A Sagittarius is also characterized as a gambler, workaholic, or miser. The native loves independence, freedom and rebels against any pressure. The archetype (Sagittarius) cannot hide feelings or opinions. At times the native is restless and undisciplined. When sick the type has little patience but always tries to heal and help others. A Sagittarius is often a symbol of wholeness, power, control and spiritual balance and may make a strong militant-like appearance. An archetype may earn fame for his wisdom and compassion. At times a Sagittarius may tend to rise to the peak of intellectual curiosity, excel at vigorous sports, including cricket, soccer, rugby, riding, auto and bicycle racing. The native is impulsive and assertive and is often a benefactor. One of the type's positive qualities is intuition with which the individual can focus his attention and with determination can solve the problems. Often a Sagittarius's energy finds a worthy satisfying physical outlet as he/she engages in socially acceptable activities. (12: p.180)

James R. Lewis, the author of **Astrological Encyclopedia,** states that Sagittarius is the ninth sign of the zodiac. It is a mutable fire sign and positively a masculine sign ruled by Jupiter. It has a mythology. Symbolically it tends to be between half human and half animal implicit with brutality and high refinement. A Sagittarius can be crude, wild wanderer, always seeking adventures and freedom from all restraint. A Sagittarius can be reckless, irresponsible, and excessively blunt, but also quite positive on many counts. Sagittarius people can be humorous, entertaining, optimistic, prize wisdom and often make inspiring teachers. All Sagittarius endeavour upward and those who are less evolved or have less impact of the sign, they climb socially up. Those, who are more developed and possess a greater impact of the sign, they strive towards a higher wisdom, spiritual development and insight. They are very fond of physical and social activities. Lewis reckons that a Sagittarius can be defined possessing the following key words related to emotional characteristics. These are: proud, zealous, energetic, hail-fellow-well-met, cheerful, open-hearted, friendly, tender, idealistic, sincere, speculative, daring, impatient, not domestic, self-indulgent. (7: p.465-66)

Planets Transiting Ninth House

The above characteristics belong to the sign Sagittarius and have been narrated in reference to the ninth house, as Sagittarius is the natural owner of the sign and the house as well. It may also imply that if in an individual's chart the ninth house is pretty strong and is owned by a beneficial planet, most of the above referred characteristics could be implicit in the person. But when Jupiter or the Sun is the owner of the ninth house, these qualities will surely be contained by the individual. When the other planets own the ninth house, there may be a slight variance in those qualities according to the nature of the planet and its occupancy of a house. We, therefore, discuss hereunder the transits of the planets in different houses when they own the ninth house. With that we shall also try to ascertain the strength of the ninth house in the light of those transits.

Transits of the Sun

When the Sun transits the ninth house, it provides intellectual growth in the native and broadens his mental horizons. The native likes to take challenging journeys for the pleasure of mind and body. All that tracking is directed by the solar energy from the ninth house. The Sun provides its solar energy in the individual to develop in him/her the philosophy of life with religious beliefs based on definite conclusions. In order to fulfil one's dreams the native needs to be more practical and direct the intellect in the necessary tracks. Further education, in the broadest sense, is related to the ninth house, just as the third house indicates 'education in general.' It is not necessary that the native may do excellently well in the usual examinations, but it is certain that subject may drive for the expansion of the mind, which may lead him/her to develop the philosophy of life. (11: p. 274)

Most of these characteristics and events will come true, if the Sun transits in Leo, or Aries or Sagittarius and owns the 9th house in an individual's chart. In case the Sun sits in the 1st or the 5th house and owns the 9th house, it will also bestow benefits relating to the house it transits in. That is, if it sits at the ascendant, it will make the person daring, less compromising and courteous, mostly acting towards goal- oriented projects, quite successful as an administrator, a professor in higher institutions, following professions related to medical fields, a successful actor, a popular military officer, freedom loving but possessing an autocratic leaning, loving vigorous sports and outdoor games.

If it is placed in the 5th house and owns the 9th house, it makes the native highly emotionally attached with religious activities, amorous in nature, blessed with promising sons, possessing drives to attain higher education, straight forward in every kind of dealings especially in business, honest, hard working, creative, loving outdoor sports, enterprising, speculative, and effortful.

The Sun's transits in the 3rd, 4th, 7th, 10th, or 11th houses (when it owns the 9th house), may also be beneficial and provide results relating to the house it sits in. If it sits in the 8th house and has aspects from Mars, Jupiter or Mercury, it may also provide great lifeforce to the native. Except when the Sun owns the 9th and is placed in the 6th or 12 houses it may not give beneficial results to the native. In all other houses it will provide highly favourable results.

Transits of the Moon

The Moon is always a very important planet in an individual's birth chart. When it is in Cancer, which is its own sign, it becomes considerably strong. The native born with the Moon in Cancer in the 9th house tends to possess great intuitive power, which will not let the individual down most of the time. There may be frequent changes in the native's moods,

which could be alarming to others. The Moon in Cancer in the ninth house may provide attraction for travel, at times long journeys in imagination only. The subject may possess a philosophical intellect and may take moral decisions instinctively. The Moon in Cancer can always influence an individual emotionally. If it is placed either in the 1st, 2nd 3rd, 4th, 5th, 7th, 10thor 11th, house as the owner of the 9th house, it is bound to provide particular house- related favourable results.

For example, if it owns the 9th house and sits in the 10th , it may help in finding jobs in navy, air-force, jewellery, or media; if sits in the 11th it will boost up the native's finances and gains; if it sits in the 1st house, it will make the individual emotional, quite fascinating in looks, critical in attitude, outspoken to the extent to create enemies easily, not much liked by others, possessing a doubting demeanour, lucky in finding means and ways to earn livelihood, less ethically oriented, poetic temperament; if it sits in the 2nd house it may make the individual emotionally rich, make him/her chatty, may help earning good money by publishing poetic literature, good at earnings; if placed in the 3rd house it may give more number of sisters and women friends, emotionally balanced and effortful, lucky and trustworthy; if it is placed in the 4th house, it may benefit the native from mother, land and property; when placed in the 5th house, it may give more number of daughters and higher education, highly amorous and ready to making love, quite productive, develop interest in research in medical fields, especially if the Moon has aspects from Mars; If placed in the 6th house, it may not give quite beneficial results and may bestow some sort of lung -related sickness; when placed in the 7th it will give the company of a beautiful and caring partner and may be highly beneficial financially; its placement in the 8th house cannot be considered beneficial as it is in its 12th house from the 9th.

We have so far discussed the Moon's placements in different houses in relation to its ownership of the 9th house only. Therefore, we are not indulging in the discussions relating to the Moon's placement and ownership of other houses and different signs. Kindly bear in mind that the Moon by the virtue of its ownership of the 9th house and placed in either 10th, 11th, 1st, 2nd, 4th, 5th, or 7th house, will surely help the individual to boost up his/her luck in various dimensions, especially the house- related areas.

Transits of Mars

Mars is very auspicious when it is placed in the ninth house. It provides the subject with great intellectual potentiality and power of concentration. The native may enjoy the experience of further education and may attain qualification, which may be highly rewarding to the subject. The individual may possess an adventurous spirit. Even if the native possesses less money, he/she may love to travel to the end of the earth just for the sake of adventure or expedition. The native will readily accept and enjoy all kinds of challenges and will have great chance of success in the adventure. As the native tends to move forward constantly, it may cause restlessness, especially when plans are changed or frustrated. The subject needs to employ more caution in that case. (11: p.343)

In fact, when Mars is placed in the ninth house, it indicates beliefs translated into action and an active enjoyment of travel and adventure. Besides seeking out new experiences and finding gains through higher education, it also bestows a fervent religiosity providing the native restlessness that requires constant travel, sports, or outdoor activities. (4: p.230)

Since Mars owns two sign—Aries & Scorpio, ***its ownership of Aries in the ninth*** would be comparatively more beneficial, because it would own 4th also besides the 9th. It would give the native a good mansion and property- related benefits as well as happiness and abundance of love from the mother. When Mars is placed in Scorpio in the ninth house, it also owns the 2nd house, the house of hard earnings, family, speech and social contacts. Hence, it will direct the native to acquire a fortune. The native will love earning money and spending on one's family. It makes the subject outspoken and sexually passionate. When Aries rises in the 9th house, Mars's placements in the 10th, 11th, 1st, 2nd 3rd, $4^{th.}$ and in the 5th house are beneficial and will provide benefits relating to that house.

For example, it will help finding jobs in acting or art- related areas when placed in the10th; financial benefits through jewellery or forest- related business when it is placed in the 11th; highly malefic and mitigating luck and fortune when placed in the 12th house; a forceful and dashing personality, love for outdoor sports and military or police- related jobs when placed in the 1st house; may involve in gambling, earning money through hard work, and be outspoken when placed in the 2nd house; possess a couple of brothers, indicates an early death of the mother and makes the native effortful and music loving when it is placed in the 3rd house; provides great benefits from mother and property and social contacts when it is placed in the 4th house; provides science-related higher education and intellectual growth leaning towards religion. It may give a couple of good and daring children when placed in the 5th house; highly beneficial financially, provide benefits through business partners and destroy enemies when placed in the 6th house; may give an outspoken and courageous demeanour, good and caring partner who may suffer from long- term blood-related sickness when it is placed in the 7th. Its placement in the 8th house may not be much helpful and make the native prone to accidents and injuries from time to time.

When Mars is in Scorpio and owns the ninth house, it also owns the 2nd house. It boosts up one's luck and helps to gain through own efforts and competitive spirit. Mars, when it is placed in the 10th house, gives medical, military, police- related jobs and provides leadership abilities in the native. When it is placed in the 11th house, it becomes highly beneficial as it is in its exalted sign and bestows financial gains through business and service. The native is affluent and rich like a king and respected in the society as their leader and benefactor. When it is placed in the 12th house, it mitigates the native's luck and makes him/her spendthrift. When it is placed in the 1st house, it gives the native gifts of imagination, sensitivity and intuition, which often manifest in creative activities. It may also be a problem creator for the partner's health and bestow a discrete disposition. When it is placed in the 2nd house, it makes the native effortful to earn a lot of money by hard and honest work. It may also give an impolite speech unpleasant and hurting to others. When it is placed in the 3rd house, the native is candid in speech disclosing his/her intentions and determination. The native is quite persuasive and aggressive in his approach to get what he/she wants to achieve. Such a native takes quick decisions, especially in emergencies. Such placement of Mars makes the native own transport business or makes him/her a dealer of communication material, a doctor, wholesaler of material concerning art and stage, a reporter or a political leader.

When Mars is placed in the 4th house, it makes the native live far from his birthplace or hometown. This placement often makes the native very effortful to improve the home conditions. Since Mars aspects the 7th house from the 4th, it may provide an uneven family life inflicting some kind of health problems to the partner making the family life difficult. Mars placed in the 5th may give only one son who may become unruly and fugitive and less attached to the parents. The native may pursue higher studies in science and may take more than usual time to complete the studies. Mars in fifth house may make one impulsive in love but possess a personal magnetism that attracts others. This sort of placement makes the native highly competitive in sports, as such, a native possesses natural athletic skills. The native may be implicit with urgent sexual need to seek for a romantic partner. Such natives can make good physical education teachers, good athletes and sculptors.

When Mars is placed in the 6th house, it indicates mechanical ability but the native may find difficulty in getting along with the co-workers. The native often chooses a vocation, which requires him/her to work with tools or machines. Mars often bestows upon the native skills to become a mechanical engineer, steel worker, surgeon or an equipment operator. In fact, Mars in the

6th house makes the native impatient with the petty things of life. But the native is a sturdy and enthusiastic worker too and gets through his/her daily routine of work. Mars in the 7th house makes the native highly independent, making him/her usually impulsive and aggressive. This placement indicates more than one marriage or more than one business partnership. Mars in the seventh house can be quarrelsome, mainly as it is impulsive. As Mars directly aspects the ascendant, it gives the native an aggressive and ego- ridden attitude, which may affect the subject's popularity and mitigate his/her social status. When Mars is placed in the 8th house, it may bestow a strong sex drive in the native and lead to unhealthy relationship with the partner. It may also affect the partner's health adversely and, thereby, may not permit to develop good relationship with the partner causing a desire to have extra- martial relationship.

Transits of Mercury

The ninth house was once considered as 'the house of dreams', therefore, the individuals with Mercury in this house may be dreamers who are capable to realize their dreams fully. Such an individual has an attraction for travel, which is connected with the native's desire to run away from living in one kind of environment for long and a fascination to know more about the distant land and people. In fact, Mercury in this house is both adaptable and exploratory. The native is very eager to gain further knowledge and meet new people. With the desire of great deal of travel the native becomes eager to learn about foreign lands and cultures and wants to understand over time the development of social ideals and attitudes, which determine people's outlook and values. When Mercury owns the ninth house, it provides intuitive, intellectual and philosophical qualities in the native. (4: p.230)

Like Mars, Mercury also rules two signs—Gemini and Virgo. Let us first briefly examine the characteristics implicit in these two signs as in any case they are going to affect the native's disposition, luck and nature. Like the nature of the Twins a native, in whose chart Mercury is in Gemini, may be convincing, persuasive, sarcastic, fickle-minded, and cunning. A Gemini always loves to invent. The native is adaptable and never afraid to try something new, which can lead him/her to be unreliable or ungrateful. Twins, the sign of Gemini, are endowed with flexibility and adaptability because this is a mutable sign, which means changeability. A Gemini individual often doesn't give too much attention to things, not because he/she cannot, but because too much else is going on. A Gemini person is charming, witty, generous, and genuinely interested, if one tries to meet the native on his/her ground—wit and imagination. (4: p.64-65)

Purity, perfection, and practicality are the values that are attached to the sign Virgin. The sign is also identified with analyzing and examining everything in details so as to improve the self and the world as well. It means serving others more than own self. It would mean serving the greater good and for that reason an individual, born with the rising sign Virgin or if Mercury transits in Virgin in his/her chart, is bound to be a responsible person. Virgin can see things clearly and work constantly for refinement. Thus, Virgo-dominated individuals necessarily try to achieve perfection. A Virgo individual may look calm from outside and may fool someone, but inside the individual is all restless full of energy, persistently seeking, improving and fixing whatever needs to be fixed. Virgin is also identified with one of the zodiac's liveliest mind tending to solve problems, possessing methodical efficiency and bent to attain beauty and perfection. A Virgo individual is practical and resourceful too. The native might agree with you when he/she senses that you are not going to change your mind but, in fact, the native wouldn't change his/her mind unless it suits his/her purpose. A Virgo individual can change by giving up the narrow views and bestow love and other important things to those who require them. (4: p.76-77)

When Mercury transits in Gemini in the ninth house, the sign Virgo rises in the 12th house. It may not be quite a beneficial placement as the 12th house is the house of waste, travels and expenditure. Therefore, it may mitigate the native's luck and diminish opportunities of progress and growth. Mercury placed in the 10th house may provide job opportunities. When it is placed in the 11th, it may give gains through the strokes of luck, offering job opportunities in media, theater, stage, teaching, and communication area. When Mercury is placed at the ascendant, it may bestow artistic qualities. The native may possess writing and sketching abilities. Mercury in the first house may cultivate mental alertness and help the native to thrive on intellectual challenges, likes to travel and loves meeting people. The native may become a great communicator and be eloquent. Mercury in the 2nd house provides gains through one's own efforts. This placement is good for engineers, mechanics, military personal, and for all those who possess strong initiative for business. Mercury being the owner of the ninth and placed in the 3rd house makes the native witty and optimistic. This placement indicates a great deal of travel and bestows ability in writing. Since Mercury placed in the 3rd house has a direct aspect on the 9th house, it tends to bestow good luck and success in business, provides good job opportunities, indicates change of jobs, and promotions. When Mercury transits the 4th house, it indicates a good early home life, help as well as encouragement from the parents, change of residence, a comfortable home environment with lots of communication going on. When Mercury is placed in the 5th house the native is often attracted to intellectually or mentally stimulating romantic partners, who are caring and wise to keep the family happy. Such a native is capable of dramatic self-expression, and cultivated in speech and writing. It also indicates a teacher of primary and middle grades. Mercury in the 6th house may help the native to grow as a perfectionist, keeping worried for unnecessary matters, quite systematic and efficient. This is supposed to be quite a favourable placement for people working in teaching, writing, healing, medicine, science or engineering and publishing. When Mercury is placed in the 7th house, the native seeks an intellectual companionship and loves a lot of verbal give and take. This placement of Mercury is a very social one and the native should seek an intellectual and well-educated partner to live happily in life. As Mercury has its direct aspects on the 1st house from the 7th, it tends to develop high communicative ability in the native and help finding jobs in media, teaching, sales departments, public relations, counselling and communication areas. When Mercury is placed in the 8th house, it may cultivate interest in occult areas and develop talent for research and analysis. The native may be secretive and highly equipped intuitively. There is also indication that the native may have sudden money-wise gains from the death of a near relative.

Mercury in Gemini in the 9th house may bestow great benefits to the native by providing him/her the ability of communication, intellectual and writing capabilities. The native will especially be successful in media, teaching and writing. Since Mercury also owns the 12th house where Virgo is transiting, it certainly mitigates native's luck to some extent by thwarting opportunities in the areas mentioned hereabove.

When Mercury transits in Virgo in the ninth house, it also owns the 6th house, which naturally belongs to it. As such, it helps the native to develop great communicative abilities. He/she is highly intellectual and is fond of travelling. The native tends to be highly analytical and is always ready to present the facts very methodically. He likes to be a professor and feels extremely happy to work in media or communication- related areas. When Mercury is placed in the 10th house, it is in its friend's house. The native with this placement has intellectually stimulating careers and is often fond of writing or to work in a communication department. He/she can also be associated with high level political leaders. Mercury in the 11th house tends to possess a wide variety of friends, often based on intellectual connections. The native has a great social status. He/she is idealistic and original. Such a native is interested in open exchanges of information with others and is dedicated frequently in humanitarian causes, science, astrology or occult knowledge, and persistently tries to achieve these goals. When Mercury is placed in the 12th house, it may tend to make the native lazy and withdrawn, unsocial, curt in behavior, spendthrift and a wanderer without purpose. When Mercury is placed in the 1st house (ascendant), it may provide great intellectual power and bring him/her luck through research and analytical abilities. The native is an excellent communicator, an orator and dedicated to work, earns his livelihood with hard and honest work. The native is likely to change several jobs, as he/she is very ambitious. Mercury placed in the 2nd house makes the native speak gently and his/her persuasive abilities are immense. Such an individual likes to convert ideas into financial gain. The native belongs to an established family and earns money with honest means and ways. He/she is very practical and true to his/her words though speaks little.

When Mercury is placed in the 3rd house, it may give more number of sisters and tends to develop good relationship with friends and brothers. It also affects the native's working quality positively and makes him quite popular with the co-workers. Such a native possesses a lively and inquisitive mind, and is versatile in handling projects. The native has a quick wit and a good sense of humour. Such a native is always eager to learn more. Such individuals may be writers, speakers, reporters, editors, teachers, travel agents and great communicators. When Mercury is placed in the 4th house, it tends to provide changes in one's residence, anxiety towards mother's health, slight delays in purchase of vehicles and frequent travels; when it transits in the 5th house, it stimulates the native to keep the company of educated and intellectual people, may give a couple of daughters, cultivate artistic tastes and love for music; when it is placed in the 6th house, it indicates high intelligence and helps the native to acquire specialized skills and knowledge for the work. The native always tends to keep up with latest research or new techniques. This is quite a beneficial placement for the individual who is working in publishing, medicine, science, engineering, printing and communication. When Mercury is placed in the 7th house, it tends to make the native successful in legal matters, and cultivates a deep desire to have the company of a highly educated partner and friends. Such a native always likes to seek mental companionship. Mercury in the 8th house may develop a desire for occult knowledge, research and analysis, may boost up the native's luck after 32 years, and create a suspicious nature and a constant feeling of unfulfilled dreams as well.

In fact, Mercury's ownership and transit in Virgo in the 9th house is comparatively better than its ownership and transits in Gemini. It is bound to augment native's luck at the age of 32 and provide him/her a great success either as an engineer, a publisher, an orator, an inventor, or a writer and give him/her a highly developed, intellectual and analytical mind, which can transform situations in his/her favour or in the direction the native feels good.

Transits of Jupiter

In fact, Jupiter is connected with physical and intellectual expansion and associated with the attainment of knowledge. It certainly helps to develop a philosophical outlook on life and encourages subject's understanding of foreign lands and people. Its positive influence makes the people optimistic and broadminded with which they direct their mental energies very positively. But when its impact is waning, it encourages blind optimism, extravagance, desire for gambling, and over developed sense of drama. (11: p.349)

Jupiter as the ruler of Sagittarius and Pisces can bestow upon the native tremendous good luck and fortune when it owns the 9th house. When transiting in Sagittarius as the owner of the 9th house, it also rules the 12th house. When it transits the 9th in Pisces, it owns the 6th house. In any case Jupiter's ownership and placement in the ninth house can give great expansion of the inner-self of an individual and cultivate in him/her a spirit of adventure and spiritual growth. It makes the native jovial and a happy-go-lucky person, full of enthusiasm and optimism. It can make him/her an explorer who always desires to seek new territories. Such an individual is extremely daring and fearless. It also tends to develop in

the native intuitive faculties and an immense desire to help the needy.

When Jupiter transits in Sagittarius and owns the ninth house, the planet's influence is strongest here for this is Sagittarius/ Jupiter house. The subject will possess considerable intellectual potency. His/her outlook on life is very positively implicit with a great wide vision. The native's imagination is generally enhanced and fired with love for travel. The individual gets opportunity for the acquisition of knowledge and to further his/her studies. When Jupiter is placed in the 10th house, dramatic flair (showy) is always present in the native. If the native is in a position of power, he/she possesses fairly good understanding and show kindness towards the subordinates and companions although he/she may be arrogant at times. Jupiter's very positive aspects on the 4th house bestows on the native great love and protection from the mother. The native possesses a great mansion and owns lands and property. The native's aspirations are high and are likely to be achieved. Successful actors and actresses often have this placing. The native possesses great ability for law, publishing and teaching or for any job he/she likes to take. When Jupiter is in the 11th house, the native may have a large circle of friends and serve on several committees in an important position. The native's humanitarian side is very strong, as such, a native constantly fights against injustice and social discrimination. It is also a great house for one's gains and advantages, which come to the native as a result of good luck and unprecedented opportunities. Jupiter's placement in the 12th house may not be as yielding because it tends to develop extravagance, wastefulness, a philosophically negative attitude towards life, withdrawn tendencies and liking to work alone. Such a native is not much known by the people. Quite often the native is not able to take decisions and, therefore, he/she is hardly able to reach the end points.

When Jupiter is placed in the 1st house (ascendant), it is a very positive placement, as it is in its friendly house. The closer Jupiter is to the ascendant, the stronger is its influence. When Jupiter is within 8 to 10 degrees from the sign of the ascendant, its influence is colossal. It provides a strong and positive outlook on life, which is likely to be lived to its full. The native is warm-hearted and optimistic, and possesses a vision of considerable breadth. Such a native is open and honest and accepts others at their face value, unless they show craftiness or display deception. The native needs to guard himself/herself against hangovers and a tendency to put on weight. Such natives tend to take jobs as surgeons, professors, military personal, lawyers or any independent business where they are at the helm of the affairs. When Jupiter is placed in the 2nd house, it tends to create an urge to earn good money. The native is often soft spoken and his/her conversation is full of wisdom. He/she loves to spend on the family whom the native cares a lot. When Jupiter owns the sign Sagittarius in the 9th house and is placed in the 3rd house, it rises in the sign Gemini. It makes the native extremely effortful. He/she takes any intellectual challenges with great pleasure and enthusiasm and loves to exercise the mind to reach the success. This position provides the individual great ability to communicate and a constant desire to continue learning even after completing the school. Jupiter sitting in the 3rd has its full aspects on the 9th house. As such, it brings great luck to the native. It definitely inclines his thoughts to spirituality and provides job opportunities that involve a lot of travelling and communication.

When Jupiter is placed in the 4th house, it indicates a happy childhood and a positive relationship with the parents. In this placement Jupiter is likely to bestow gains through land, vehicle and parental property. Jupiter is likely to influence the native's imagination positively and create love for travel. When it is placed in the 5th house, it may bless the native with able and gifted children who would be devoted to the parents. The native is likely to be highly productive in the field of his/her work, and is full of great enthusiasm and optimism having a leaning towards spiritual and religious activities. When Jupiter is placed in the 6th house, it tends to create love for food and may indulge the native in bad eating and drinking habits. The individual tends to be showy than to be practical. He/she may often be a daydreamer and a boastful individual with little output and more wasteful thinking. When Jupiter is placed in the 7th house, it tends to develop high expectations from the partner, and may not be so lucky to have a partner of his/her choice. Hence frustration may ensue and disruption may occur in relationship with the partner, unless Venus is well-placed in the chart. When Jupiter is placed in the 8th house, it may provide a great lifeforce and physical strength, which may be more sex- oriented and demanding to the partner. The native may tend to be more aggressive in his/her day-to-day life and lack a good social status. It is also possible that in this placement Jupiter may make the native indulge in metaphysical imagination relating to death and life after life.

When Jupiter transits in Pisces and owns the ninth house, it is a very lucky placement as it has its full aspects on the ascendant (1st house) where the sign Cancer is rising. Jupiter in Cancer is sympathetic towards people, and possesses a highly compassionate disposition. The native has a good sense of humour and has an optimistic outlook. Jupiter placed in Cancer at the ascendant provides the native honestly earned money. The native is highly affluent, prosperous, socially acclaimed, and loved and respected widely. When Jupiter is placed in the 9th house, the native is enthusiastic, energetic and sympathetic. He/she is generous and passionately involved with philosophy, foreign cultures, distant travels and higher education. Jupiter in the 10th house bestows an independent spirit, a courageous disposition, and possesses a natural quality of leadership. Such a native is often innovative, possesses great enthusiasm and is highly ethical. When Jupiter is placed in the 11th house, it gives riches and social status. Such an individual often indulges in great social service and humanitarian activities, as he/she possesses earnest love for the people. He/she is artistic, emotional and inclined to love fancy things. Jupiter in the 12th house transiting in the sign Gemini provides the native highly communicative abilities and spendthrift nature. At times it tends to decline or delay the native's luck. Jupiter in the 2nd house makes the native large-hearted and self-confident and radiates charm, warmth and generosity. It inspires the individual to think big and, at times, he/she has flair for drama as well. But ultimately Jupiter makes the native grow thoughtfully. Jupiter in the 3rd house is highly practical and helps the native to attain great ends. Such a native grows pragmatically, loves travelling, writing, publishing, cultivating friendship with highly literate people, and is highly effortful. Jupiter placed in the 4th house makes the native believe in conventional moral values and provides a strong sense of justice.

The native is always honourable in dealing with others. In this sign Jupiter makes the subject grow socially but he/she is quite dogmatic and tends to change residence often. When Jupiter is placed in the 5th house, it cultivates a great love and attachment towards religion, children and moral values. The native possesses a strong desire to gain wealth and to grow powerful in all respects. When Jupiter is placed in the 6th house, it makes the native heavily interested in philosophy, belief system and higher education. It also tends to develop in the native some sort of illness from time to time and, consequently, frustration and disappointment ensues. Since Jupiter transits in its own sign in this house, when it rules the 9th house as well, it ultimately provides strength and strong will to attain success the native aims at. In the 7th house Jupiter transits in its debilitated sign and, as such, it tends to develop less agreeable relationship with the partner, but it certainly tends to make the native magnanimous and thoughtful, ready to help the needy and the poor. Jupiter in this sign often makes the native socially acceptable. When Jupiter is placed in the 8th house, it tends to provide new ideas, great intellect and makes him/her implicit with impartiality. Jupiter in this placement (Aquarius) makes the native strongly believe in a world without class, race and religious distinctions. The native loves travelling and spends on the needy. Jupiter placed in this house endows the individual with a strong lifeforce with which he/she is determined to fight impediments that come in life. At times such a placement of Jupiter makes native rich and provides him/her financial benefits from some nearest relatives.

Transits of Venus

Besides Jupiter, Venus is another planet in the zodiac system that exerts beneficial influence on an individual if wellplaced in the chart, though it is not as big or strong as Jupiter. Venus exerts its influence the way we are related to other people both socially and economically. Individual's attitude to money and possessions are also the concern of this planet. Traditional astrology reckons that Venus has to do much with one's partner. If it is wellplaced in a chart (kundali) and has aspects from friendly planets, it is bound to give a caring and a loving partner. It would also accelerate one's financial status. Let us examine its various placements when it owns the 9th house. Like Mars, Mercury or Jupiter, Venus also owns two signs—Taurus and Libra. We shall now discuss the placements of Venus in different houses keeping in view its ownership of the ninth house in a chart.

When Venus transits in Taurus in the ninth house, it also owns the 2nd house. As such, it brings financial gains to the native and gives him/her a sweet tongue with which he/she is able to arrest people's attention, love and respect. There will be great need and desire for travel, especially to foreign countries, where a couple of romantic episodes may occur influencing the native's life and routine. The native is wisely relaxed and possesses philosophical leaning towards life. The individual loves to live in an idealistic world, which is beautiful and serene. It is, in fact, a very lucky placement of Venus in a chart. When Venus is placed in the 10th house, it tends the subject to develop good relationship with colleagues, who love and respect him/her. It is a good placement for a native who is desirous to work as a teacher, a media person, a lawyer, or wants to pursue an independent business relating to restaurants, food and garments, and in related areas. When Venus is placed in the 11th house, it makes the native highly emotional, social, and caring for the other people. If the Moon is wellplaced in the chart, it is certainly going to provide great financial gains to the individual. This placement of

Venus is likely to give the native a great many friends who would not only admire and but also bestow love on him/her. When Venus is placed in the 12th house, it may mitigate luck and develop a tendency of spendthrift. The native may not be able to pursue his/her goals and suffer on account of frustration and failure. But the native may tend to grow in spiritual field and try hard to lead a disciplined life in later years. When Venus is placed in the 1st house, which would be its debilitated sign, it provides a considerable charm and attraction in the native. He/she would move very gracefully and is socially desirable on account of his/her kindness and compassion for people. Such a placement may also make the native a schemer, a liar, a conspirator, lucky, easy going, showy, desirous to gain money even by fraudulent means, an artistic, a writer, a columnist and a voracious reader.

Venus's placement in the 2nd house is considerably lucky, as it transits in its own house. It provides the native aesthetic pleasures and material security. The native possesses great love for beauty and tries to look good to attract others' attention. It also provides a tendency of possessiveness, especially fancy things and art-related material. The individual may also have great interest in music, drama and aesthetic activities and find vocation in these areas too. When Venus occupies the 3rd house, it has its full aspects on the ninth house. As such, it helps to develop the native's ability to communicate and extend sympathy towards others, which tends to extend his/her social circle and status. It also makes the native very effortful, lucky and not wanting in jobs. The native may like to choose teaching, art-related jobs, love writing, publishing, directing, acting, and likes to take up jobs relating to the aforesaid areas. When Venus is placed in the 4th house, the native may take great pride in the home and would be keen to make it look beautiful and comfortable. The native is likely to extend great love to the immediate family, parents and relations, which may be frustrated at times on account of too much emotionalism and attachment. The native is likely to change a couple of residences and jobs during his/her lifetime. When Venus is placed in the 5th house, it may cultivate an amorous learning in the native. The individual may fall in love several times and choose a partner who is senior in age and more matured physically and emotionally. This placement of Venus also cultivates a good habit of reading and writing. The native may publish books and articles and may find job in media. When Venus is placed in the 6th house, the native may tend to love rich food and drinks and there may be a possibility of gaining weight. The native will be easily critical of others incurring their displeasure and dislike. Such a placement of Venus may incur some sort of health problems and disturb good relationship with the partner. He/she may be lazy and would not enjoy working hard. When Venus is placed in the 7th house, it will be in its exalted sign. As such, it may bestow benefits from the partner, who would be highly talented and artistic in nature besides being a caring and loving person. Both, benefits from the partner's company and financial gains through the partner, are quite likely when Venus is placed in the 7th house from its 9th house ownership. This placement may also subdue the native's identity because the partner may be so charming and dominating. When Venus is placed in the 8th house, it may increase the intensity of individual's emotions and cultivate feelings of jealousy. A strong Venus in this house may give a great life force to the native and may provide a rich sex life too.

When Venus transits in Libra and owns the ninth house, it is an excellent placement. Venus bestows high ideals and an admiration for high culture. The native may possess a great understanding of foreign people. This placement also indicates that the native may merry a foreigner or spend one's life abroad. Since Venus also rules the 4th house when it transits in Libra in the ninth house, it does provide home- related benefits, love and benefits from one's mother and acquisition of great property, which may provide financial benefits to the native. These financial gains are certain when Venus as the owner of the 9th and 4th sits in the 11th house, which is the house of financial benefits. When Venus sits in the 10th house, it might bestow a career relating to arts or cultural work, which may give the native prosperity and social status. The native being socially popular might use his/her influence to gain public positions. This placement indicates counselling, diplomatic relations, and high position in art- related departments could be possible careers for the native. When Venus is placed in the 11th house, it indicates lots of friends and associates of both sexes. Venus in the 11th house may provide tastes for music, fashion, art and culture. It's a great placement of Venus as regards individual's social status is concerned. Venus placed in the 12th house indicates a private routine of life of the native. An individual with this placement of Venus has a great desire to serve others in some way and often looks at life's deeper meanings and finds an outlet through his/her devotion to God. Such an individual is noted for secretive love affairs or personal contacts. He/she is also known for his/her love for travelling long distances and possessing a spendthrift disposition. When Venus is placed in the 1st house, it indicates beauty, harmony, grace, kindness, friendliness and unusual charm in the native. This placement indicates not only physical beauty but also possible artistic talents. A strong Venus in this house indicates a happy childhood leading to a positive and hopeful outlook. When Venus is placed in the 2nd house, it indicates financial advantages through partnership and a tendency of spending on clothes and pleasure. Such a native is honest in the financial dealings and might seek wealth through attaining social positions. When Venus is placed in the 3rd house, the native is often a compromiser and seeks harmony through communication. It also indicates artistic creativity, love of literature, music and travel for pleasure. The native loves reading, writing, publishing and creating inspirational literature beneficial for self-growth and self-help.

We have already discussed Venus's placement in the 4th house. When Venus is placed in the 5th house, it is both light-hearted and emotionally objective. In this placement Venus likes intellectual encouragement and romance as well. The native possesses a tendency toward lack of commitment and he/she is far too lighthearted to stay in one place for a long time. The native may possess a tendency to flirt. The subject may cultivate good literary talents, great love for language, and indulge in social activities too. (Madeline G-B Lisa L. p.146) This placement of Venus may give more number of daughters than sons, but most children might do well in education and artistic fields. Venus in this placement certainly helps developing love for communication. When Venus is placed in the 6th house, the native tends to nurture love and care for others. It is a good placement for counsellors, health care-workers and jobs that require artistic pursuits or social areas connected with women's welfare. Venus in this placement may provide fairly good health, still the native needs to take good care of health for he/she might possess a tendency to overeat. More intake of sugar may also develop sugar- related illness. When Venus is placed in the 7th house, it tends to develop passionate love for the partner. This placement can be very successful in legal matters and the native gets along very well with everyone. Such a native shows good ability to deal with the public and works successfully in sales, areas relating to arts and public relations. The native tends to have a love for self-expression and a talent for the dramatic, but is often generous and selfless. Natives in this placement of Venus in their 7th house are often open-minded, are passionate in love and love fine things as well. When Venus is placed in the 8th house, the native cultivates social, emotional and artistic values. He/she is more sincerely affectionate than any other sign. The native often looks for and finds sexual fulfilment and quite likely inherits money from a near relative or a loved one. Excessive sexual indulgence needs to be checked for it may lead to health problems and unsocial activities leading to public apathy.

Transits of Saturn

Saturn is all about one's responsibility, rules and regulations. It is mainly concerned with one's self-discipline, self-respect, duties and limitations. When one grows older, Saturn also represents one's own authority. Saturn represents individual's ambitious side so it is well aware of one's weaknesses and strengths. Saturn always reminds us that as social beings,

we must abide by certain laws that are both earthly and universal. Saturn also rules two zodiac signs—Capricorn and Aquarius. Saturn in Capricorn is very ambitious and persistent and wants to succeed. There is a pretty good chance that it will succeed as it is hardworking and disciplined. In Aquarius Saturn wants to run the whole show. It desires both freedom and order. Saturn in Aquarius in an individual's chart can manifest very well but the native must learn to set oneself free from its excessive pressure to achieve both freedom and order.

When Saturn transits in Capricorn in the ninth house, it also owns the 10th house, perhaps it is one of the best placements of a planet in the zodiac world. It cultivates a great desire in the individual to learn. He/she carefully explores philosophy or religion. Saturn in the ninth house often seeks positions and authority, status in the field of education, religious institutions, publishing business, international affairs, law and politics, spying jobs, positions in secret police agencies and professors in universities. When Saturn is placed in the 10th house, it makes the native self-reliant, disciplined and determined. With these qualities the individual is likely to achieve great success in life. This placement of Saturn likes responsibility and, therefore, the native do very well in business or job he/she chooses. But there is a fear when Saturn is in this position that such a native might compromise values to achieve one's personal goals. Early problems with the father are likely to be converted into responsibility towards one's family. When Saturn transits in the eleventh house, it is basically Saturn's own house. Such an individual has a few strong and meaningful friends and some delays are expected in achieving objectives. Older people are often very helpful to the native. As Saturn has its direct aspect on the 5th house from the 11th, it is going to give failures in love making opportunities and thwart the individual's sex satisfying desires bringing frustration and disappointments. Saturn is also likely to inflict bad effects on the partner's health resulting in miscarriages or early death to sons. Such a native is likely to have company of senior and old people and might be benefited by them in different walks of life. When Saturn is placed in the 12th house, it may bring losses to the native through thefts or losing in shares or by natural calamities. Such natives are often very secretive and like to live aloof. Such a placement might give unfounded fears about one's own worth and ability. Such an individual is often suspicious about others and so others also look at him/her with a doubtful eye. The native has a hidden identity, which is not shared by others. Such natives often seek jobs in big companies, industries and institutions for the government and might also get chance to travel abroad in groups, or government organized trips. When Saturn is placed at the ascendant and owns the 9th house, it makes an individual very showy, cultivating lies and often compromising with values. In this placement Saturn occupies its debilitated sign, so it gives early failure in most of the tasks the native undertakes and provides obstacles to become independent and free. But ultimately it brings success to the native as he/she is used to do persistently hard work and loves responsibility. Besides, Saturn also has its full aspects on the 3rd, 7th and 10th houses from its placement in the 1st. It provides the native a good, senior and matured partner. The native gets the company of highly educated people and friends, and gets success during his/her later years of life that he/she has been wanting since long. When Saturn is placed in the 2nd house, it is bound to make the native very polite, diplomatic, eloquent but very calculative speech, good in politics and law, appreciation for sculpture and love for archives. Saturn's placement in the 3rd house makes one travel distant lands and help keeping the company of highly educated people. The native might get opportunities to work as a professor in a university and be highly honoured by the colleagues and students. Saturn in this placement certainly boosts up the native's luck but as he/she grows in age, more benefits are experienced by the subject. Saturn placed in the 4th house may develop a strong attachment and responsibility for the family because of early loss of the father. Such native often needs self-esteem and more love as in early child hood the native has experienced more difficulties.

Saturn in the 5th house often keeps the native less relaxed. Because of this seriousness in nature the native is frequently creative, especially in the fields of science, arts, politics and business management. Such a native would like to work in a business associated with investments, education, shares, education and places of entertainment. Saturn in this placement tends to give serious responsibilities concerning children. Such a native is often romantically attracted to someone older or more matured than himself/herself. When Saturn transits in the 6th house, it tends to be a good and beneficial placement. It tends to provide decisiveness and good judgment in the native and offers him/her great public careers. It helps the native to develop long- term relationship with the people and tends to make him/her successful in one's own business. It also bestows good positions in either forest departments or judiciary, or engineering, or nutrition or food and helps to build business in oil or coal areas or to have an industry connecting oil or coal. When Saturn is placed in the 7th house, it delays the marriage of the native, bestows artistic talents and a tendency of dependence on others. It is not quite a favourable placement of Saturn to benefit the native to have a caring and loving partner. But certainly it boosts up the native's luck after 32 years and goes on helping the subject as he/she grows in age by providing material benefits. When Saturn is placed in the 8th house, it protects the native from ailments, and lengthens his/her span of life. This placement also bestows some sort of sudden financial gains received through some near relatives, gains through lottery, or by some other unknown ways and means. It also makes the native quite prudent and provides clever thinking leading to act pragmatically.

The transit of Saturn in the ninth house in Aquarius is a very lucky placement for a native as Saturn owns both the 9th and the 8th houses. Saturn in the 9th house often seeks positions of authority and is interested in social stability. Its direct aspects on the 3rd house may not be quite helpful and create misunderstandings and problems with the brothers and friends and also make the native less effortful and resourceful. But as he/she grows in age it provides better insight and wisdom leading to an enhanced social position. Its debilitated aspects on the 11th house, brings financial benefits from various resources some of which may not be straight. Capricorn in the 8th house gives good luck, illness-free health guarding the native against serious diseases and accidents, sudden monetary gains and a good social status.

When Saturn transits in Aquarius in the ninth house, it provides similar kinds of benefits and losses to the native as when it transits in Capricorn and owns the ninth house except that its placements in the 3rd and the 7th may not be quite lucrative. In the 3rd house it may provide loss of brothers and sisters, bestow a lazy disposition and unintelligent approach to life's problems, and make the native less desirous to take jobs seriously. In the 7th house it may create disruption in the relationship with the partner and break that relationship as the native grows in age. But in this position it will bestow intelligence, eloquence and communicative ability. When it is placed in the 12th house, it may mitigate luck and may not provide good opportunities of success, jobs and financial gains. It may make the native a wanderer without mission leading to a financial breakdown. Its placement in the 2nd house may also not be very lucrative, as it might cultivate a sharp and biting tongue tending to create more enemies than friends, though it may provide financial benefits, if the Moon is well placed in the chart. Its placement in the rest of the houses will bring benefits, as it would have brought when placed in the ninth in the sign Capricorn.

Let us discuss some horoscopes in relation to the ninth house and ***identify certain rules to ascertain the strength of this house*** as well as discover the basic principles, which would enlighten the reader to understand what kind of placements and aspects of the planets would give strength to this house.

The Rules

1. *Any planet(s) as an owner of the ninth house if conjuncts with the owners of the 1st, 4th, 5th, 7th, 10th, 11th and or placed in any of the following houses such as (in order) 9th, 1st, 10th, 4th, 5th, 11th, 7th, 3rd, or 2nd, it will highly be beneficial and provide benefits associated with the house it sits in.*
2. *Owner of the ninth house when placed in the 12th house is bound to affect the native's luck adversely, reduce his/her financial benefits and job opportunities, constantly develop dissatisfaction and frustration in life and make him/her an aimless wanderer/traveller without money.*
3. *Aspects on the ninth house by its owner or friends or beneficial planets especially the owners of the ascendant and the ninth house, will provide excellent benefits to the native bestowing financial gains, company of great friends and benefits from sons & grandsons, advantage from a caring partner, great job opportunities, travels to foreign lands and job opportunities there, and constant prospects of higher education.*

In the light of the above rules/principles we shall present and analyze a number of charts (*kundalies*) for the benefit of the reader.

Example 1

Following is the chart of a native employed in a senior position in the Forest Department of a State Government.

Native born on 6th February, 1957

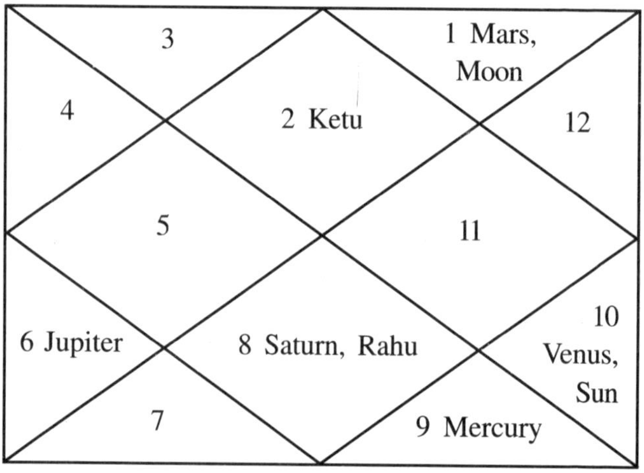

Discussions

The ninth house of the native occupies two planets, Venus and the Sun, which are the owners of the ascendant and the fourth house respectively. Besides, the owner of the ninth house Saturn, aspects the ninth house and Venus, the owner of the ascendant. Venus is a natural friend of Saturn hence benefits are immense.* As such, it has provided great luck to the native in terms of a good and a big house, personal transport, and financial affluence. Saturn's aspects of the Sun, the owner of the fourth house cannot be considered altogether positive. As a result, it has never benefited him to live in his own house for a long time until the age of forty seven years except for casual visits. It has also affected the mother's health adversely and relationship with the father is just normal. The owner of the ninth house (Saturn) aspects its own house and therefore, the native has travelled far

* Please see Appendix II to check for the natural planets and natural signs in their houses.

and wide and even outside the country. Saturn the owner of the ninth and the tenth is sitting in the 7th house wherefrom it aspects the ninth house forming a kind of *rajya yoga*. Consequently, the native got the job in the forest department (Mars aspects on the owner of the ninth, Saturn) at an early age around 22 years. ***Thus, aspects from the owner of the ninth on its own house are bound to provide good luck and yield highly favourable results.***

Example 2

The following chart belongs to a promising young Engineer visiting USA for further studies.

Native born on 1st December, 1976

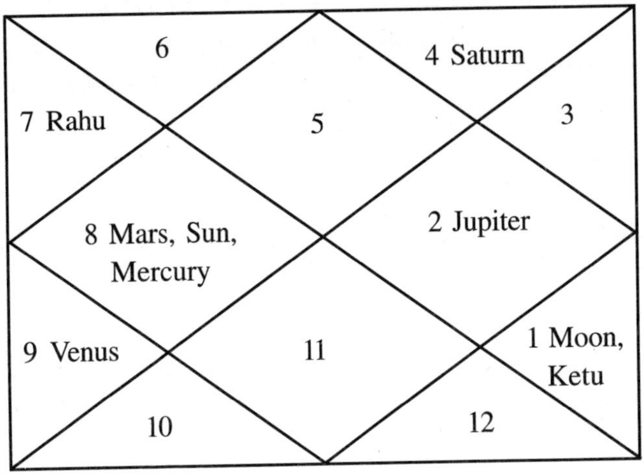

Discussions

The owner of the ninth & fourth Mars is conjunct with the owner of the ascendant and Mercury, which is the owner of the eleventh and the second houses. Since there is a very favourable conjunct (aspect) between the owners of the fourth & ninth, and the ascendant, it has formed a very strong *rajya yoga* giving the native benefit of a good house and a car at a very early age. The ninth house is also associated with higher learning. So it was during his 29th year that he got a chance to go abroad for further studies.

Besides, before leaving for USA at the age of 29 years after obtaining a B.E. degree from a Regional Engineering College four years back, the native got very good opportunities of working in prestigious car companies like Honda in India. As the owner of the ninth (& the fourth as well) is conjunct with the owners of the ascendant, eleventh & the second houses, the native will not only live in great government accommodations, but will also enjoy financial affluence. He will reside for more number of years in the north of his birth place, except for a short time when he would live in the West as Saturn's aspect on the ninth house is debilitated. Jupiter, being a natural friend of Mars and the Sun, is going to benefit the native to achieve further higher education as it aspects both Mars and the Sun.

It confirms the rule referred to here above that the owner of the ninth when conjuncts with the owners of the 1st, 4th, 5th, 10th 2nd 11th or even 7th houses, it will yield favourable results associated with the house it sits in.

Example 3

The following chart belongs to a young promising Pharmacist engaged in post-graduate studies.

Native born on 5th January, 1982

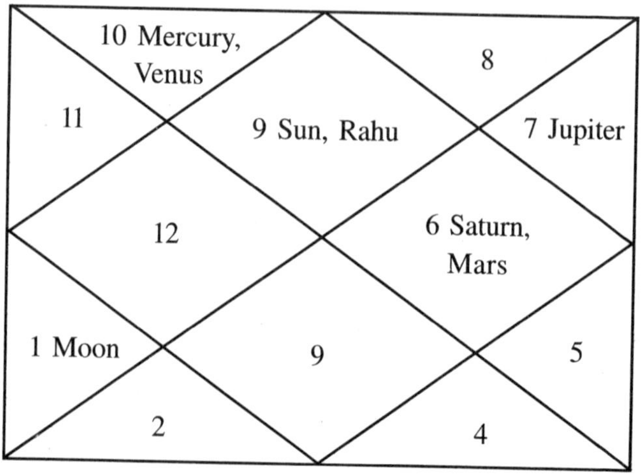

Discussions

The owner of the ninth Sun, transits the ascendant giving the ascendant great strength, energy and progressive outlook. It also helps to provide higher education and visits to foreign lands. The subject has already visited a few foreign countries when he was just one year old. The Sun in Sagittarius, which is a fire sign,* is described as enthusiastic, impulsive and spirited. Such natives are adventurous and innovative but impatient and less practical also at times. The key word for Sagittarius is 'freedom', which can lead to difficulties as well as delight. Such a native tends to lead life on his own way. He will be more than a little careless. If driving, for instance, he will drive with a sort of casual manner, which will make the passengers uncomfortable. The native tends to take risks, almost for his own sake. But intellectual pursuits will probably be quite as important to him as the physical life. The native may also love the challenge of competition.

Most of these qualities are contained in the native, who is highly enthusiastic, agile and ready to work at a moment's notice. He is enormously versatile, but he must learn to control the impulses. Otherwise, life may be full of half-achieved objects. The Sun, transiting in Sagittarius, is associated with professions like military, medical, carpentry, sports, pharmacy, teaching and archery. The native has already completed his under-graduate degree in Pharmacy and is heading for a post-graduate degree. Therefore, he has already chosen the profession he is destined. But Rahu conjunct with the Sun and Ketu's aspects on the ascendant, mitigate the benefits to be provided by the Sun, the owner of the ninth. The native needs to control his wild and aggressive impulses to make his life more meaningful. As the owner of the ninth is sitting at the ascendant, the native is likely to get further higher education and travel abroad around 27 & 32 years of age.

---

* Please see Appendix III for Refining the Signs & to understand their intrinsic characteristics as well as the elements of nature such as fire, earth, air and water, they possess as a result of being ruled by the heavenly bodies.

Example 4

The following chart belongs to a retired Principal of a Senior Secondary School.

Native born on 20th October, 1928

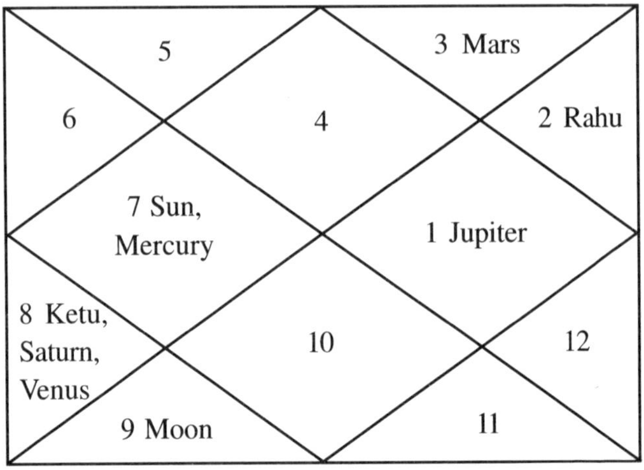

Discussions

The native was born in the Sindh province of British- ruled India and migrated to western India in 1947 with the family. Leaving some early difficulties that include the mother's ailments and her demise when the native was very young, all went on well as Jupiter the owner of the ninth protected the fourth house as well as the Sun by its aspects. But almost at the age of 15 plus when Saturn was transiting in Aries, it afflicted the Sun by its direct aspect and caused the demise of the father. But the owner of the 9th, Jupiter, was transiting in Aries in the tenth house in the chart at the time of the native's birth. It helped the subject to get a teaching job immediately after the father's death. It also gradually provided opportunities for higher education without much interruption. *Just one strong planet owning the ninth house and placed in the tenth, helped the subject to live well and to get higher positions in the government in Education Department*. Before the subject took voluntary retirement from the government job to join her children in the foreign lands, the native was already promoted to the principal's position of a senior secondary school. Thus, the owner of the ninth house provided the native higher education, foreign travel as well as good status job-wise as it is placed in the tenth, the house of karma or practical ability and professional benefits.

Example 5

The following chart belongs to a Senior Professor of History retired from NCERT, New Delhi.

Native born on 18th October, 1930

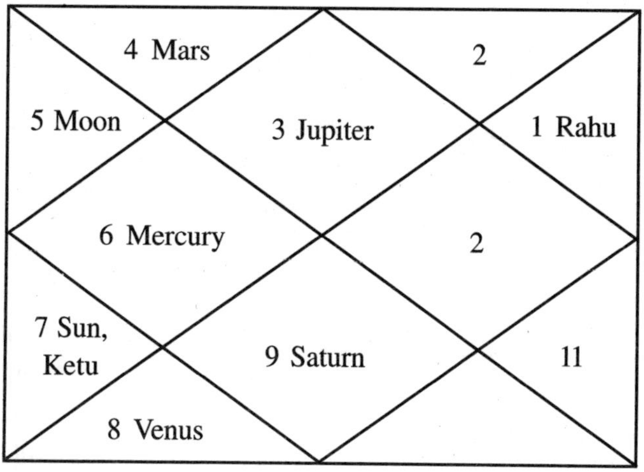

Discussions

The subject was born in the Uttar Pradesh in a royal family and his childhood was full of parental care and affection. Close examination of the chart clearly indicates a positive and constructive influence of the mother on the native's childhood. The subject received good education and went to England for further education, which is predicted by the placement of Saturn in the 7th house and its aspects on the 9th house. In fact, both the owners of 9th and the 10th have their direct aspects on each other resulting in a kind of *rajya yoga.* Besides, both, Jupiter and Saturn have aspects on the 9th house, which helped the subject to achieve higher positions in the NCERT by the time he retired. He travelled several foreign countries during his placement in the

NCERT. Thus, the owner of the ninth house, Saturn, provided the subject, both, higher education, travelling far and wide and to the foreign countries. When he was actively engaged at the NCERT, he almost travelled throughout the country (and foreign lands) as the head of a group or a member of a visiting team, which gave him great advantage in widening his professional vision, which is also a kind of higher education in itself.

Example 6

The following chart belongs to a lady teacher working abroad.

Native born on 15th September, 1960

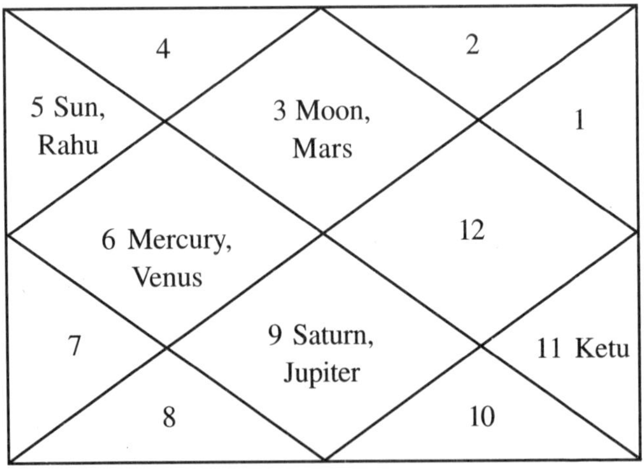

Discussions

The native was born in the western Rajasthan around forty five years back from the time this chart is being analyzed. Early education took place within the State in good schools and before completing post-graduate education in the country, the native went abroad for further studies. But before finally settling down in USA, the subject visited several foreign lands in Europe and Africa as both the parents were working abroad. Though Jupiter and Saturn's conjunct form *chandal yoga,* they also form *rajya yoga* as they own the 10th and the 9th houses respectively. As the ruler of the ninth, Saturn (conjunct with Jupiter) aspects the ninth house and Saturn also aspects the fourth house, it has not only provided opportunities to visit foreign countries, but also made the native settle permanently in the West. Saturn's aspects on the ninth has benefited the subject to get further education which the native received in the US after leaving the home country. Thus, the placement of the owner of the ninth, Saturn, in the 7th house and having aspects on the ninth itself, has benefited the native in attaining higher education and visiting various countries outside her own country.

Example 7

The following chart belongs to a promising post-graduate engineer seeking employment and desirous to go abroad.

Native born on 26th March, 1980

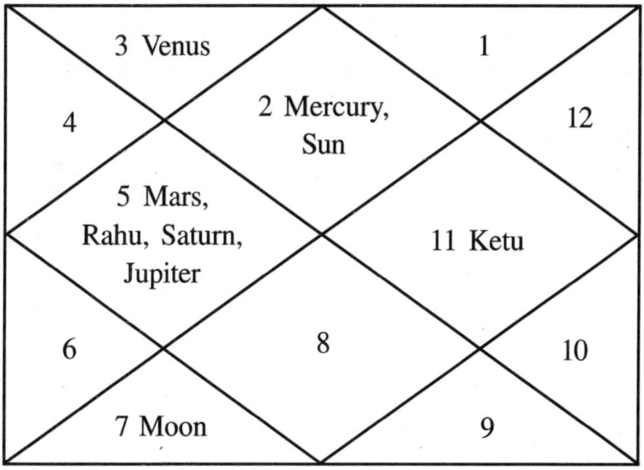

Discussions

Currently the native is only 25 years old and possesses a post-graduate degree in engineering. The native's chart possesses good rajya yoga as the owners of the ninth & tenth Saturn, is conjunct with the owners of the 11th and the 7th. Jupiter and Mars respectively. As Saturn, the owners of the ninth as well as tenth, aspects the tenth from the fourth house, it is bound to give the subject good job opportunities, and take him abroad around 29 years of age.

Saturn is currently re-transiting the sign Cancer since 8th October 2005 (subject to a slight variation of the date), as such it aspects the ninth house. It is a good placement for one and a half years to bestow good job opportunities to the native, and provide also great opportunities to travel foreign lands, including in his own country. As we are limiting our discussion to the ninth house and its ownership, we shall discuss matters relating to the ninth only.

In fact, Saturn and Mars conjunct in a good house like 1st, 4th, 10th or even 7th house are extremely favourable to make the native a good engineer and to help him possess a great insight in the profession. Except that Mars's aspects on the 7th, is not quite beneficial as far as the native's married life is concerned (unless the partner's chart has similar combinations or cancellation in respect of Mars's aspects), Mars and Saturn conjunct is very auspicious and favourable to the native.

Example 8

The following chart belongs to a Headmaster of a Secondary School in a State Government, working there for the last twenty years.

Native born on the 10th January, 1955

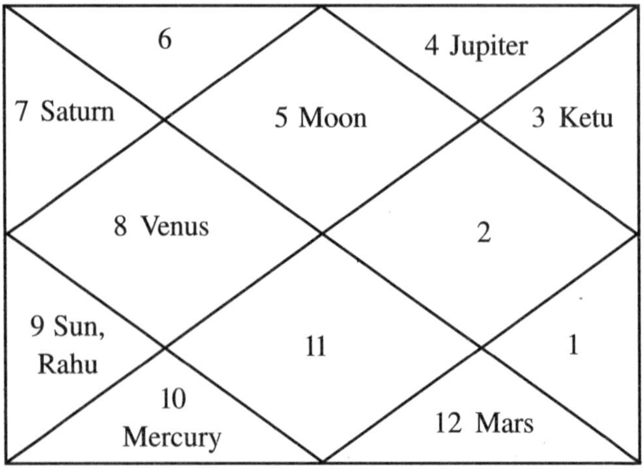

Discussions

Since the owner of the ascendant, the Sun, is afflicted being conjunct with Rahu, the native possesses a clouded thinking which has affected his early progress although he got plenty of opportunities to grow. Besides, a weak Moon (29.6 %), owner of the 12th is sitting with Jupiter, which makes the subject aggressively emotional. Since the Moon is about to move to the ascendant in a few hours, it provides a disposition that often tends to disrupt relationships with people and relatives. But the owner of the 9th Mars (sitting in the house of its natural friend, Jupiter) has a direct aspect on it from the exalted Jupiter. It has provided the native good luck and opportunities to grow, although the native's ascendant is badly afflicted by Rahu. Venus has also a direct aspect on the tenth, which is its own house.

Both these planets (the owners of the ninth and the tenth) have restored much of the opportunities lost by the native in his early life. Job-wise the native has reached a respectable position and possesses quite a good social status as Jupiter is sitting in the 12th house in its exalted sign. Although both, the ascendant and the owner of the ascendant are afflicted and possess ill aspects, the owners of the ninth and tenth houses by their good aspects on their own houses have restored a lot of luck and provided benefits, which an afflicted ascendant would have never provided to a native. ***Therefore, the owner of the ninth plays an important role in a subject's progress, social status and financial affluence.***

Example 9

The following chart belongs to a lady Professor highly educated and currently working in a privately owned Law college at a State capital.

Native born on 14th November, 1961

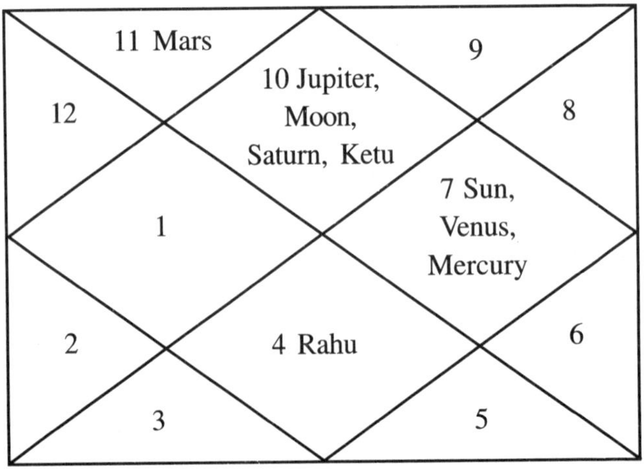

Discussions

The above chart presents an excellent example of a native's good luck in view of favourable placement of the owner of the ninth house. Not only Saturn, the owner of the ascendant has strengthened the 10th house by its exalted aspect, the owner of the ninth Mercury also transits in the tenth house making it stronger. Besides, Venus, the owner of the tenth, is also conjunct with Mercury its natural friend in the tenth. The Sun, owner of the 8th also provides a great life-force to the native in the tenth house. As such, the ninth house owner's role has been accelerated in favour of the subject.

The native has excellent record of education and possesses a Ph. D. degree in Law. Currently the subject is employed in a leading privately- owned Law College and has been working in the capacity of the Head of Department. In view of the planets' placement, and the owners of the ninth, fifth, and the seventh being conjunct in the tenth house, it is expected that the native will soon get a better opportunity of promotion or jump as a Principal of the same College or elsewhere.

It is also quite possible that the subject may shift to another Law College after one-and-a-half year. *When Saturn transits in Leo after one-and-a-half year from the time this analysis is being made, it may benefit the native further by providing more and better job opportunities in Government setup or else where, except that Saturn's transit may not be very favourable to the subject's father. Since the owner of the ninth is conjunct with Venus, the owner of the tenth and ascendant, Saturn, has an exalted aspect on the owners of the ninth & the tenth, there is a possibility that the native may travel abroad also.*

Example 10

The following chart belongs to a very senior ENT medical doctor working in a state government hospital.

Native born on 6th January, 1955

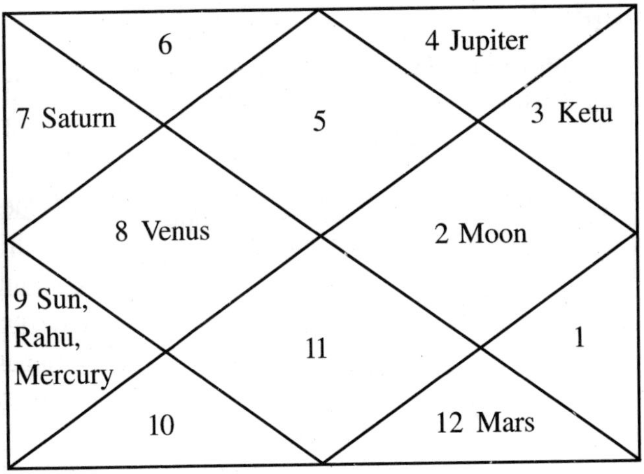

Discussions

The above chart of a senior ENT medical doctor, is another example when the native's ascendant, the Sun, has been afflicted by Rahu, but the owner of the ninth house has turned the tables in favour of the native. Its direct aspects of the exalted Jupiter on Mars, the owner of the ninth house, has restored much of the missed opportunities. Besides, an exalted Moon, though the owner of the 12th house, sits in the tenth house and has direct aspects from Venus, the owner of the tenth house. It is definitely a positive placement leading to beneficial results except much financial benefits. One more planet has its aspects on the ninth. It is Saturn, which has its debilitated aspects on the ninth house. As a result of that, the native has not been able to get adequate recognition in life although as an ENT doctor he is far too good. He has often been transferred to places without much of his liking. Although the native is good in his field, financially he does not get much benefit from his clients as his own disposition and interest is not to earn money. ***In fact, it is mainly the owner of the ninth that has brought the native much academic success and expertise in his field, since it has aspects from the owner of the fifth. It has helped in reducing the ill effects of the ascendant being conjunct with its natural enemy, Rahu.***

Example 11

The following chart belongs to a prospective Chartered Accountant, who is struggling hard to settle down in his profession.

Native born on 16th September, 1979

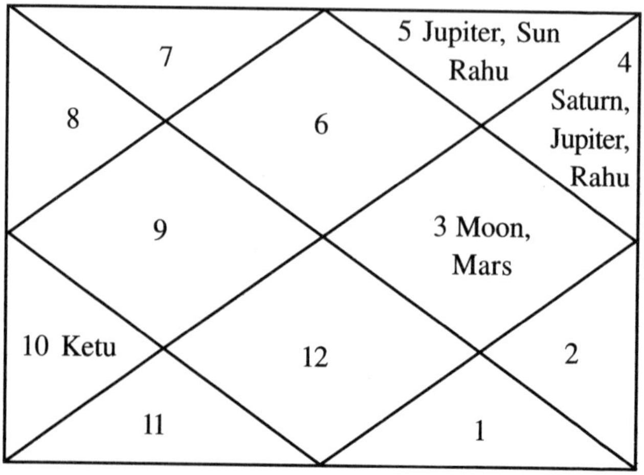

Discussions

The native is currently studying for his CA and has not been successful in the last two attempts to clear his examinations. Let us once again examine the position of the ninth house for assessing the benefits from the ninth house. The owner of the ninth, Venus, is sitting in the twelfth house with its natural friend Mercury, which also happens to be the owner of the tenth house. Thus, the owners of the ninth & tenth are placed in the twelfth house, which is the house of waste and expenditure. Consequently, the native's efforts are being wasted. Besides, both Venus and Mercury are combust with the Sun. Therefore, the owner of the ninth, which is responsible for higher education is unable to provide any benefits to the native. However, Saturn's currently transiting in the sign Cancer (September 2005- Fbr. 2007), may provide some benefits to the native to attain some success in that direction. Besides, Jupiter's transit in the sign Scorpio after August 2007 may bring some benefits to the native in completing his mission. ***Let us, therefore, keep in view that the owner of the ninth if placed in a good house as well as in a good and friendly sign, it is bound to provide very good results. But if it is placed in the 12th, or 6th houses and transits in its enemy house or in its debilitated sign it would not bring any benefits to the native.***

Example 12

The following chart belongs to an Assistant Commissioner in Military Finance Setup in the Central Government.

Native born on 10th January, 1969

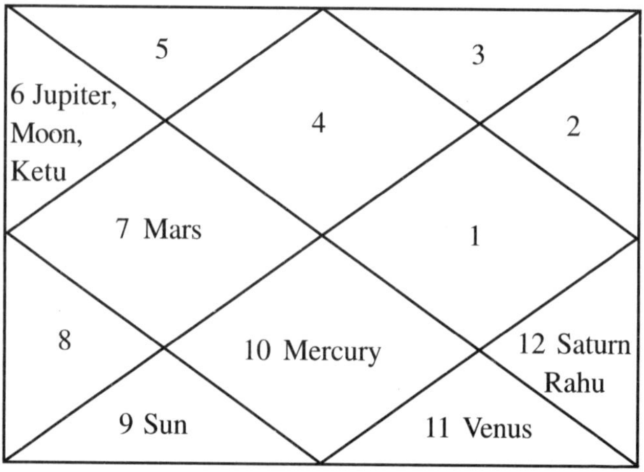

Discussions

It is also a very clear example of a native whose owner of the ninth house is placed in the 3rd house and has aspects on its own house. As a result, the native cleared his higher education in the field of Chartered Accountancy well in time and opened a private office at his home for several years with great success and financial benefits. But as the owner of the 10th house Mars, is looking at its own house, it inspired the native to apply for IAS Services. The native appeared for the concerned examinations for a couple of times with not much success although he passed the written examination every time. Ultimately, when Jupiter was transiting at his ascendant around three years back from the time this analysis is being made, it looked at his 9th as well as 5th houses. He finally got success. But instead of getting his posting in the Revenue Department, which his other members of family had desired, he got his placement in the Military Setup.

Thus, one must keep in mind that the owner of the ninth if wellplaced and if it aspects its own house, it is bound to bring the desired benefits to the native.

We conclude our discussion relating to the ninth house and implore the readers to keep their minds open and read as many horoscopes as possible to achieve better understanding of the planets aspects, placements and conjuncts. If the practising astrologer whether a beginner, has an open mind (is objective), and stays on the scene constantly, there is a pretty good opportunity for him/her to develop a clear insight & understanding about astrology. Besides, to learn astrology better one must go deep into the unexplored fields of knowledge and try to find out further facts in the areas that have been taken for granted since long. Astrology, in our opinion, is such a vast and deep field of knowledge that the more one digs out of it the more one would achieve.

✡ CHAPTER FOUR ✡

The Fifth House

House of Romance, Children, Sports & Creativity

The fifth house in the Western world is associated with creativity, fun, romance, risk, sports and children. Traditionally, Indian astrologers consider it mainly connected with children, productivity, creativity, and education. According to Krishnamurti Paddati this house is related to children, productivity and romance too.

Creativity is not simply related to the arts. One may be especially creative in a boardroom, kitchen, in writing, painting and any other field. Julia and Derek reckon creativity is often stimulated by one's parents and this house is concerned with parents' feelings about their relationship with a child. The fifth house also has a strong association with pleasure, particularly with regard to one's attitudes about love affairs, the act of love, and having children—that means with all the ways one translates emotional and spiritual love into physical form. (10:p.111)

Madeline G-B Lisa Lenard considers that as the fifth house is related with creativity, it is, therefore, natural that this house would encompass children, risk-taking and romance—all creative and risky endeavours. It is also the house of investments, another risky area. The natural ruler of the house is Leo and is associated with the planet Sun. If one wants to find out how much creative one would be in life, he/she needs to study the fifth house. The fifth house indicates one's pleasure, fun, parties, vacations, self-indulgence and self-expression. It includes everything from gambling to holidays and besides romance one could think it as the house of joy and the heart. The sign related to the fifth house indicates the nature of one's creativity and articulateness. Its ruler indicates how and where one develops one's abilities to express oneself. The house where Leo, its matching natural sign lies, shows where one's creativity and purpose are released and what area of one's life will provide the native the creative potential. (4:p.209-10) The fifth house, the house of play, describes the ignition point of joy behind art, sports and spontaneity. It is also about the simplicity of presence, of just being. Of creativity, the fifth house says: *Be it and, therefore, birth it.* The creative child is conceived in joy out of spontaneity, and so the fifth house rules children. The fifth house sponsors the space to love life, moment by moment, and those with the Sun in the fifth house tend to be warm personalities who shine particularly brightly. (1:p.150-51)

Characteristics Accredited

Before predicting the effects of the transits of various planets in the fifth house, we would like to identify the basic uniqueness contained in the sign Leo, which is recognized as the natural owner of this house. Most of the characteristics are drawn from the nature and personality of lions. Thus, Leos are self-confident, bold, dramatic, strong and creative. Like lions Leos are expected to be at the head of the line—implicit with pride.

Leos don't give up like a lion chasing its prey until he gets it. Self-expression and creativity are everything in a Leo and it is his/her will power with which a Leo person creates in his/her life. Eventually, the native learns to follow more than just his/her own will aligning oneself with the higher Self and the creative principles of the Universe. As Leo is a fixed sign, a Leo can be determined, inflexible, persistent or even habit-bound. A confident Leo individual is born to lead and is proud, courageous and self-assured to a fault. A Leo native can be generous, commending, ambitious and proud. This means the native can also be intolerant, demanding and self-righteous. A Leo person can lead others to tremendous victories but can be pitiless to the enemies. But Leo native's memories are short, therefore, he/she is quick to forgive. A Leo person often likes to be surrounded by yes-men. This in turn leads to lack of caution and hence he/she is flattered easily. A Leo individual is extremely loyal and expects loyalty in return. A generous Leo expects generosity in return to his/her sincerity. As the native is loyal, it becomes difficult to end relationship with him/her. A Leo being in love provides love to others and like a king graciously loves to give to the people who are loyal to him her.

In human relationships, the Leo personality is thought to harmonize with Sagittarius and Aries with whom he/she establishes a reciprocal companionship. As friends, Leos gather a number of acquaintances, but they have only a few bosom friends. Before choosing a mate or a partner a Leo individual is said to have numerous affairs and may live in attachment before finally selecting a lifetime companion. A Leo may have failures in love but the subject gets healed soon as he/she has a great trust in future. A Leo's level of confidence is great and so he/she renews the faith in the self at a great speed. (12:p.134)

Home is another place where a Leo's generosity is evidenced. Every kind of guest is welcomed and all friends are loved to come home. Most Leos love to be leaders and like to preside at every occasion but some would like to be teachers to provide enthusiasm to their students. A Leo individual always loves to have audience and feels good to take up jobs where he/she can have people to listen to him/her. The areas of work where a Leo can do well are sales, teaching, consultancy, tour guiding, management and performing at the stage as an actor or a leader. We would like to consider now the transits of the planets through the fifth house.

Transits of the Sun

The Sun in the fifth house is energetic, strongly creative and loves to live the good life. The native has interest in art, likes to be with people and is happy to have a free hand with money. The Sun placed in this house loves to enjoy every moment of time. The native loves children and others too. Since self-expression is one of its traits, the native finds it through teaching, acting, art, sports other kind of artistic pursuits. Natives with the Sun in the fifth house are very loyal, great lovers, always ready for action, and mostly project themselves stylishly and with a sense of drama.

When the Sun transits in the fifth house in Leo, it will give the native a couple of good sons excelling monetarily and attaining a great social status. The native's ambitions will be very strong and at times he/she may also indulge in showing off. As this is the house of children, the subject would like to push the children to the forefront. The native will tend to take emotional and physical risks and may involve in gambling, if the Sun does not have good aspects on it. If the Sun is placed in the 9th house, it will provide great luck to the native, provide colossal opportunities for higher learning, and a great drive for the expansion of mind will also be present in him/her. The solar energy of the Sun will give the native great opportunities to visit foreign countries on government assignments. Possibility of a good partner cannot be ruled out when the Sun is placed in the 9th house. When it is placed at the ascendant, it will provide great social status, a commending and leading position in the government or any business concern and recognition in as a great scholar. Such a native possesses a great self-esteem and commands great respect from the people. When the Sun is placed in the 6th house, it tends to provide illness and make the native worry about the general health. The sense of duty and routine is also emphasized by this placing. When the Sun is placed in the 8th house, it provides great lifeforce and agility to excel in the field of work. Sexual satisfaction will be a powerful outlet for self-expression. Deep purposeful force and great emotional intensity are shown in this placement of the Sun. It is, therefore, essential that the powers of intuition must be controlled. When the Sun is placed in the 3rd house, it benefits the native with immense communicative abilities and makes the subject highly effortful. When it is placed in the 2nd house, it tends to cultivate artistic ideas and the native's imagery is full of aesthetic innovations. The native seeks great plans for self-expression and finds ways to convert those ideas into action in the field of art and culture. It also accelerates his/her desire to amass wealth and riches. When the Sun is placed in the 4th house, it may give benefits relating to property and land but also bestow loss of one of the parents. The Sun's placement in the 12th house, though in a friendly house, mitigates the native's social status on account of arrogant and aggressive disposition and bestows lack of will power and confidence. But ultimately it might lead the native to seek the Divine. Its placement in the 11th house is financially beneficial, but it may disrupt relationship with the children. When the Sun is placed in the 7th house, it may not permit the native to marry early or create disorder in relationship with the partner. This placement often suggests conflict with the partner or disappointment and unhappiness in love, but its aspects on the ascendant will provide great status, success and benefits from the children. Its placement in the 10th house may be good in respect of job opportunities and bestow upon the native great practical ability to do innovations and research in the fields of technology and science. It is a great placement for attaining personal objectives successfully.

All the above benefits and losses will be enjoyed by the native in view of the good and bad aspects of the planets on the Sun. Planets, like Jupiter, Mercury, and Venus, are likely to provide good results but aspects from the Saturn are likely to mitigate the good effect of the house in which the Sun is placed in a chart. One more thing needs to be kept in mind at this juncture. ***It is about the retrograding of the planets***. When planets retrograde, they don't provide exactly the same results, which they would have given when they are in regular procession. When the planets retrograde, their effect on the house where they sit and where they have aspects changes in some way. Please see our explanation in this respect in the **Appendix IV** given at the end.

Transits of the Moon

When interpreting the influence of the Moon and its sign position, one must remember that the subject will intuitively and instinctively react and respond to all those attributes in the manner of that sign. The Moon is strongly associated with 'feminine' qualities in a birth chart and is related with maternal impulses, parental influences, compassion, nurturing instincts, imagination and domesticity. The key words associated with the Moon are responsiveness, instinct, intuition, fluctuation, and emotions. The Moon has its strongest influences on an individual's psychological makeup and approach to the world. (Julia & Derek Parker, Parker's Astrology, p. 284 ; & Guide to Astrology, p. 261) The Moon's main concerns are individual's emotions, intuition and feelings. Thus, analyzing one's chart the reader must keep in mind some of these aspects of the Moon.

When the Moon is placed in Cancer in the fifth house, it indicates an active and a happy disposition. The native may be overwhelmed with ambitions and it powerfully heightens the native's overprotective tendency in all situations. It is a good placement to exhibit the native's creative ability mainly directed towards procreation of children, with great joy gained through children. It also tends to develop artistic or poetic talents, which the native may like to exhibit through writing and publishing. It is a great placement of the Moon to express one's love towards the opposite sex and try fulfilling it to a great extent. The Moon in this placement may provide more number of daughters than the sons. When the Moon is placed in the 6th house, it may have ill effect on the individual's health and create constant worry in that respect. Like the Moon, the native's health may go through phases. The native must adhere to the diet rules to keep oneself healthy and devoid of illness. In this placement the Moon indicates frequent changes in jobs and it affects the native's working capacity too. The Moon's placement in the 7th house may tend to express one's emotions towards the partner unevenly. If the Moon has beneficial aspects on it, there may be a considerable balance in exhibiting one's emotions towards the partner. Hence it may lead to a considerably positive relationship with the partner. A seventh house Moon is usually popular with others, mainly because the native is very sensitive and responsive to the needs of others. The native may marry early in life and the partner may be moody, sensitive or emotionally changeable. But the Moon's aspects on the ascendant may develop an emotional but trustworthy disposition towards friends and the partner. When the Moon is placed in the 8th house, it is more concerned with intuition, emotion and deep-rooted feelings. It is quite likely that the native may possess a 'sixth sense' especially when Jupiter, Mercury or even Venus aspects the Moon. If the Moon has Mars's aspects, it may provide a great lifeforce and unending energy for work. The subject may also possess excessive sex desire which needs to be fulfilled but if it is not fulfilled it may lead to frustration and unsocial conduct. (11:p.291) In this placement the Moon has a deep-seated need for security. The native is often interested to find answers to the questions about death and after life. In this placement the Moon provides instinctive understanding of others' needs and wants. Such a native often has changeable circumstances involving intimate relationships. This placement also indicates occasional hurts and small accidents subject to Mars' aspects on the house.

When the Moon is placed in the 9th house, it is likely to provide good luck to the native. It also indicates that the native's religious and philosophical beliefs are tied to the past or parental conditioning. The native may get great happiness from travelling and journeys and broadening experiences can create further development of his/her beliefs and ideas of reality. This placement of the Moon tends to develop a highly imaginative and receptive mind and there is also a high consciousness of the supernatural in the native. The native tends to be a natural teacher and feels at home in jobs relating to navy or jewellery-related business. When the Moon is placed in the 10th house, the native may be secretive, and would be prepared to sacrifice the private life for the attainment of success. Such a native is favoured by the public and is often successful in politics and careers that deal with public. In this placement the Moon has a direct aspect on the 4th house. It indicates a good home and extremely good relationship and a long life to native's mother. When the Moon is placed in the 11th house, it helps the children to acquire good jobs but it also indicates uneven relationship with people and the children. The native is more popular with the women folk and has more female friends. When the Moon is placed in the 12th house, the native is sensitive, emotional and intuitive and can be easily hurt. The native may possess a deep desire to live in seclusion and like to meditate to attain spiritual goals. The native often possesses tendencies to escape from the pressure of work and from the public eye. He/she tends to spend emotions on trivial matters and gets unhappy on matters of insignificant nature.

When the Moon is placed in the 1st house or the ascendant, it indicates imaginative self-expression and a deep desire to be admired and appreciated by others. Such a native is steadfast and possesses a strong determination. The native's judgments and reflective capabilities are strong and lean towards the truth and reality. All this will be true, if Jupiter is wellplaced in the chart and has its aspects on the Moon. The native's personal identity is often influenced by his/her early childhood and family. The subject has often strong ties with the mother. When the Moon is placed in the 2nd house, it is a very strong placement as far as possessions and money are concerned. This placement indicates a great ability to earn money from business associated with food, homes, and real estate but his/her finances may go through phases. It also indicates an emotional disposition as far as the native's speech is concerned. When the Moon is placed in the 3rd house, it indicates great communicative qualities. The native is often effortful but will have changing phases in making efforts. The subject may have more number of sisters and women friends who will be helpful in the native's career. Such a subject may take jobs relating to media, publishing and teaching. Touring jobs will highly be profitable. He/she will love to go on pilgrimage and may devote quite a number of years of life in religious and spiritual pursuits. When the Moon is placed in the 4th house, it indicates a strong parental attachment. The native identifies emotionally with both family and home, especially with the mother, who is often a benefactor to the subject. It is quite possible that the native may possess a great property and land, if Mercury is wellplaced or has its aspects on the Moon.

Transits of Mars

Mars influences our physical energy levels, assertiveness and sex drives. Mars also shows how easily we are roused to anger because it governs the flow of adrenalin in our body. Mars influences our competitiveness, initiative and boldness. The planet is also strongly associated with how aggressively we interact with everyday world—both physically and verbally, especially when encountered with conflicts, which require our quick response and immediate solutions. When Mars is placed in a negative sign or in a less beneficial house, it rules our explosive and violent disposition and encourages hasty decisions and unruly conduct.

When Mars transits in Aries in the fifth house, it is extremely active and rewarding love life. Besides, it is likely to provide an additional emphasis on sexual pleasure. The native is often an assertive lover who desires to take the lead and who always wants a good response from the partner. The native is often positive in lovemaking and tends to take pleasure in children. Such a native will have a risk-taking tendency and perhaps he/she may have something of a gambling spirit. Mars in Aries will bestow a powerful physical energy, which the individual will often express very positively. In fact, the native's sex drive is powerfully increased by this placement of Mars. This placement also increases the desire for parenthood. Such an individual is usually uncomplicated and would like to reduce the complex problems to a few simple components. When Mars is placed in Aries, it provides a great flow of energy, which makes the individual engaged happily in varied interests. (11:p.335) In fact, the native is an uncomplicated person in just about every thing. If he/she is devoted to sports, which is a very strong area of interest for the native, he/she may excel in the field of his/her interest to a great extent.

When Mars is placed in the 6th house, it may develop weak and unbalanced sex drives. The native is somewhat short of passion. The native may be edgy and tense, restless and nervous and need continual activity to release the tension. The subject may tend to be impatient with petty things of life. Though the native may be a sturdy worker but he/she gets through the routine with a sort of distasteful precision. That may cause stress resulting to develop a tendency to suffer from skin complaints, with rashes or allergies, causing constant annoyance. At its best Mars can add determination, firmness and the ability to work very hard at career, spare-time interests and hobbies. Mars in this placement may also lead to love dancing. When Mars is placed in the 7th house, the native desires romance, love and harmony in the relationship with the partner. One of the planet's effects will be to encourage the native to fall in love with at first sight. The native tends to be versatile and energetic and does not find time to get relaxed. The native also wants variety and experimentation in his/her sex life. The subject is very keen to make the partnership work still there may be many quarrels and disruptions in the relationship with the partner. Seventh house Mars often suggests separation or hard time with the partner. When Mars is placed in the 8th house, it tends the native to have strong sex drives, which needs to be expressed in a positive way. In fact, in Cancer Mars has a distinct and powerful influence on the sex life. The subject is a sensuous lover who knows just what pleases the partner most. In this placement Mars develops in the individual a caring tendency to turn possessive. But Mars's aspects on the 2nd house from the 8th house, makes the native highly effortful to earn money and to be very curt and impolite in speech. When Mars is placed in the 9th house, it is in a very strong position, as it owns the 5th house. With this placement Mars tends to make the native a good organizer and a leader.

The subject expresses his/her emotions very positively and he/she really loves life. The native does not have petty mindedness but his/her temper is quick and blows up out of nowhere. It is a very luck placement of Mars that helps the native grow steadily and gradually and takes him/her at the top at an early age.

When Mars is placed in the 10th house, it tends to create in the native a lot of desire and emphasis to have a good career and a successful professional life. Such a native is sharp in mind and can be argumentative and intolerant to the people with slower minds. As Mars owns the fifth house, it is bound to make the native mentally strong in his/her professional career trying to excel in his/her career from the others. In this placement Mars aspects on the fourth house may help the native to possess good land and property but it may create some problems for the mother's health. Mars while sitting in the 10th house also aspects the 5th house. It may help the subject to possess a couple of bright children and inspire him/her to publish material, especially in the fields of science, gardening, forestry, or chemistry. When it is placed in the 11th house, it inspires the native sexually active and often makes him/her fall in love at the first sight. Such a native is often highly independent and tends to be cool and detached. But he/she has a great enthusiasm for the social life that makes him/her a leader in the social area. Mars in that placement has a full aspect on the fifth house. As such, it gives him/her an intelligent son who will be caring to the parents. This placement may also help the native to publish material especially in the field of science. When Mars is placed in the 12th house being the owner of the fifth house, it may cause disruption to the native's educational career, loss of children and lead individual's thinking to spiritual and religious direction. It may also cause a jealous and revengeful disposition that may cause disruption in the relationship with the partner. In this placement Mars may also develop spendthrift tendencies and the native may spend a lot of money in unfruitful travelling too. Mars's placement in the 12th house often makes the native arrogant and aggressive in disposition causing problems with the partner and friends.

When Mars is placed in the 1st house being the owner of the 5th house, it is helpful in respect of career and inspiration to get a good position in life. It also makes the native's thinking spiritually motivated but in this position Mars is often detrimental to the relationship with the partner unless its placement in the partner's chart is also beneficial. However, in this placement Mars gives a great boost to the physical and mental energies of the individual and makes the native quite versatile. It also helps the subject to possess good property, if Jupiter is also wellplaced in the chart. When Mars is placed in the 2nd house, it has a commending placement, as it has full aspects on the fifth and the ninth houses. Thus, it tends to bestow beneficial results relating to children, writing and publication, foreign travels, and love for sports. It will also be financially lucrative. The energy from Mars will direct the subject to acquire a fortune. The native enjoys his money and is pleased to spend it and also happy to have others to spend it with you. Its aspects on the eighth house may cause small accidents and get hurt below the waist but if Jupiter is wellplaced, its ill effects may be nullified. This placement of Mars makes the native possess great endurance, which is obviously an advantage in some jobs and leisure activities. The native becomes highly ambitious and the planet spurs him/her towards the objectives. The subject copes well with any risks but unlikely to be foolish to take unnecessary risks. This placement also tends to make the native a good athlete. When Mars is placed in the 3rd house, it makes the native quite inquisitive to find answers to any questions that occur to him/her. It tends to create a kind of eccentricity, which does not permit the native to take any work seriously although this placement of Mars makes the native quite effortful. However, its good aspects on the ninth house, ratifies much of the laziness eccentricity and make him/her productive. Mars's placement in the 4th house may provide mixed results. It is beneficial job-wise and may help him/her to earn money and be socially popular, but it may be detrimental to the health of the partner and delay the marriage until 28th years of age. That ends the discussions on the placement of Mars in various houses when the sign Aries rises in the fifth house. Let us examine Mars's placement in different houses when the sign Scorpio rises in the fifth house.

When Mars transits in Scorpio in the fifth house, it is one of its best placements, as besides owning the fifth it also owns the 10th house, the house of hopes, progress and responsibility. The tenth house reveals how well the native gets on in the world—not only just financially, but also in terms of fulfilling one's aspirations. Therefore, this placement of Mars would not only provide a couple of very able sons, a highly romantic family environment, a loving partner, constant productivity in the shape of writing and publications, but also give a great sense of responsibility and authority, abiding by the traditional values and possessing a great social status. Mars's placement in the 7th house may tend to disrupt relationship with the partner (if the partner's chart does not contain beneficial combinations or aspects relating to the 7th house), but it will certainly provide a good political and social status, great job opportunities preferring a high position in medical, military, police, engineering filds or forest department and financial affluence. Mars placed in the ninth and the tenth houses when it would own the fifth house, will highly be beneficial as it will bestow great job opportunities and also give opportunities to travelling foreign countries on government assignments. Its placement in the eleventh house will provide great social status and good relationship with wellplaced women in the society, and cultivate artistic tastes bestowing talents of acting and stage direction. In the 12th house it may bestow conversational ability and develop interest in expanding knowledge about religion and spirituality. It may also lead to be linked with hospitals, prisons and mental institutions, and all such places where one can experience deep loneliness. When placed at the ascendant, it may give an aggressive, egoistic and critical disposition, but it is a good placement job-wise. Its placement in the 3rd house may make the native highly communicative and effortful having the company of literate friends and loving brothers. Its placement in the 2nd house may bestow cultivation of frank speech and a deep desire to earn money. In rest of the houses Mars' placement owning the fifth house in Scorpio may bestow similar benefits or losses what it would give when it owns the fifth house in Aries.

Transits of Mercury

Mercury's influence on humans might appear meager, but Western astrologers now believe that the planet is a powerful agent of self-knowledge. Mercury symbolizes flexibility overcoming rigidity. Thus, Mercury is the supporter of a new beginning, upsetting traditional attitudes leading to inventions and change. Indian traditional astrology always considered Mercury as a strong agent to influence human conduct, luck and wisdom since ancient times. Mercury tends to provide the message of personal transformation and to bridging the gap between the self and its potentials. In fact, the expression *mercurial* refers to people with lively and changeable temperaments. People born under Mercury's influence can be experts in finding out others' intentions. Mercury may bestow argumentative, critical and sarcastic attitudes in a subject. It also denotes the gifts of great perceptivity, intellectual versatility and skills at communicating knowledge. If there is strong positive influence of Mercury on a native, it tends to bestow the quality of transforming words into substance. The planet is strongly related to the art of procuring information and communication. The natives who have strong influence of Mercury can successfully work either as journalists, teachers, travelling agents, secretaries, carpenters, engineers and doctors or pharmacists. The planet rules the signs Gemini and Virgo and relates to thyroid, nervous system and intellect, as well as senses of sight, hearing and touch. (Cosmic Connections, p.42) Let us discover the effects of Mercury when it owns the fifth house in Gemini and Virgo and transits in various houses.

When Mercury transits in Gemini in the fifth house, it develops great communicative ability making the native highly creative and productive. Mercury in Gemini is full of ideas and tends to bestow on the subject agility of mind, wit and charm. It is an inquiring and communicative mind that wants to know. In the fifth house Mercury always tends to bestow feelings of love, desire to change and to be intellectually stimulating to keep the good times rolling. In this placement the planet may provide the capability of dramatic self-expression, especially in speech and writing. The native might work as a schoolteacher, a writer, an art critic or a stock market analyst. Mercury in the 6th house may be quick to pickup everyone's signals and the individual is as good a receiver as a communicator. Such a native often possesses an intuitive mind, a good memory and strong poetic talents. The native is often good in understanding the importance of details, especially about the matters relating to health and wellbeing. The subject may tend to have unnecessary worry about trivial matters, but will possess great intelligence and acquire specialized skills and strong knowledge for work. Such an individual is often systematic, efficient and possesses a strong desire to conduct research on the latest problems and techniques. It is a very favourable placement for the native who is working in medicine, science, engineering or healing fields. When Mercury is placed in the 7th house, it tends to make the native outspoken and optimistic, dramatic and idealistic. This placement of Mercury makes the individual creative. He/she is likely to keep good and emotional relationship with the partner with occasional skirmishes but soon healed as the native is inclined emotionally towards the partner. The seventh house Mercury seeks intellectual compatibility in both marriage and partnerships. This placement can benefit the native in the fields of law, literary pursuits, and communications. Besides, jobs like public relations experts, counsellors, and mediators can also be suitable for the individual. (4:221) Mercury's aspect on the first house from its placement in the seventh house may provide dramatic talents and career in acting, film-directing, printing, publishing and teaching. When Mercury is placed in the 8th house, it provides a logical mind, which is good at precision. Such a native is highly analytical, practical and quick at learning new things. Mercury's placement in this house provides talents for research and analysis. The native is often interested in occult knowledge and is intuitive, secretive and psychic. Such natives are likely to know the true motives of others and are highly capable to dig out others' secrets. In this placement the native is often interested in corporate finance, taxes, insurance, research or writing on mystery or occult topics. When Mercury is placed in the 9th house, it tends to bestow a balanced mind but the native is quite diplomatic, charming and wellbalanced. Mercury in the 9th house is both adaptable and exploratory. The native is always desirous to gain further knowledge and meet new people. This placement involves a lot of travel, develops interest in higher education and learning foreign cultures. It also bestows a great interest in philosophical knowledge leading to dogmatic beliefs at times. The native is often highly communicative, effortful and loves seeking jobs in the fields of media, publishing, teaching, research and analysis, and politics. When Mercury is placed in the 10th house, it bestows the capability of knowing the real meaning behind the words. It makes the native critical and quick to judge. In fact, Mercury in this placement is a proving mind, one that can reach the heart of the matter. In this placement Mercury bestows the talent to communicating ideas to others in variety of ways. Such natives have intellectually stimulating careers related mostly to writing or communications. Educational opportunities received by such natives facilitate them to achieve significant social status. Such natives are often associated with high level political leaders, or become distinguished lawyers or speechwriters. With this placement Mercury at times provides the native a status of a great political leader known for innovative ideas. Mercury may bestow opportunities to the natives of travelling and change of jobs as well. In this placement Mercury may provide a loving and highly caring mother and good property as well. Such placements are helpful in taking up jobs as lawyers, professors, criminal prosecutors and art critics attached to media. When Mercury is placed in the 11th house, the native loves to learn and is quick to explore, but he/she does not like to stick to anyone idea for very long. As a result, the native is often unable to pursue projects to their finish. Still the native desires to seek the truth and wants to follow the problem to quite a good length. In this placement Mercury provides opportunity to have a wide variety of friends based on intellectual relations. Such a native is often social minded, idealistic and original who loves to participate in group activities. Such natives love to dedicate their time in science projects, humanitarian causes, study of astrology or occult knowledge, and are quite persistent in reaching the goals. When Mercury is placed in the 12th house, it makes the native contemplative and provides ability to analyze other people's problem successfully. Mercury in this placement provides an original mind. Such a native is often a hard worker and a practical person who often utilizes the attained knowledge for practical purposes. But it may also make the native spendthrift both in money matters and speech, which can adversely affect the native's social status by creating more enemies than friends.

When Mercury is placed in the 1st house, it provides a great quality to grasp abstract ideas enabling the native to understand peoples' motives. In this placement Mercury provides an open mind and scientific approach to achieve new discoveries. In fact, in this placement Mercury leads one to possess an inventive mind, which starts with original ideas devoid of traditional influence. When this placement occurs the native is mentally very alert, loves to travel and enjoys meeting new people. The native is a great communicator, quite often secretive, loves public positions, socially accepted and likes jobs relating to law, teaching, media, and administration in education, editing, publishing and participating in political activities. Such a native may possess quite an imposing and charming personality that can easily captivate others' attention. This placement may also be quite wholesome for the relationship with the partner unless Saturn has adverse aspects on the seventh house. When Mercury is placed in the 2nd house, it helps the native to earn money through communicative abilities. As such, he/she may like to take jobs relating to teaching, writing or in any areas that deal with public matters. Such a native will possess good lifeforce that will provide him/her agility to work and to be highly productive affecting positively native's capacity to earn.

When Mercury is placed in the 3rd house, this placement makes for a lively and inquisitive mind trying to be first in everything. This placement may also mean a premature and a headstrong nature possessing spontaneity and a desire to take immediate action or running ahead before it gets all the facts. But if Mars is placed favourably in the native's chart, it may make the subject highly productive and provide good company of friends who are wellplaced in the society. This placement can also lead to restlessness and may develop liking for professions relating to writing, reporting, editing and dealing with public speaking.

So far we have been dealing with Mercury's ownership of the fifth house starting with the sign Gemini. When Mercury is placed in the 4th house, it makes the native's imagination implicit with art and culture- related ideas. In this placement Mercury is likely to be helpful in getting property and good benefits from a very caring mother. Its beneficial aspect on the 10th house is likely to provide good job opportunities in the field of teaching, research, editing, writing, publishing or media.

When Mercury is placed in Virgo in the fifth house, it may give almost similar results what it would provide when it owns the fifth house in Gemini, except that it may be aggressively romantic, highly productive in communication and writing. The native will also be extremely caring and loving for his/her children, and like to keep the company of the women or literate friends and a partner who is emotionally agile and reciprocates love. Its placement in the 11th house may bring great benefit from the children and writing ability, but native's social status could be affected in some way, as the planet would be in its debilitated sign there. Its placement in the 9th house would bestow great luck, agility and excellence in producing innovative ideas leading to new findings and inventions. In the 12th house Mercury would give a doubting mind which may not possess highly productive imagination. Its placement in the 4th house may develop less concern for the parents, especially for the mother, bring frequent changes in residence and job transfers, and may provide a dogmatic disposition which may give a narrow vision as far as comprehending the reality is concerned. Job-wise it may be moderately a better placement, if the Sun is placed in a beneficial sign in the chart. Mercury's placement in rest of the houses will bestow almost similar results what it would give when it owns Gemini is the fifth house.

Transits of Jupiter

Huge and majestic Jupiter generates more radiation on its own than it receives from the Sun. Thus, it forms the center of a miniature solar system of sixteen moons. Jupiter is said to inspire us to reach beyond our immediate circumstances, spiritually and materially. It is there fore associated with justice, benevolence, compassion, religion philosophy, law, honesty, wealth and social status. Those native in whose charts (*kundalis*) Jupiter predominates, they are respectful and may flout traditions in the name of higher principles. They have a tendency to over generalize, and tend to throw broad concepts or ideas without much examining them. Such natives are completely optimistic. People in whose chart Jupiter is placed in a beneficial position, especially at the ascendant, they would like to choose jobs as scientists, philosophers, pastors or priests, judges, philanthropists, teachers, chief executives, and lawyers. Such natives often possess an aristocratic deportment and language traits suitable to diplomats. Jupiter rules Sagittarius and Pisces. Let us discover in what manner Jupiter influences individuals when it rises in Sagittarius or Pisces in the fifth house and transits in different houses when it owns the fifth house.

When Jupiter is placed in Sagittarius in the fifth house it owns the eighth house also. In this sign Jupiter provides far-sightedness. Consequently, it helps the native to act upon the opportunities he/she receives in life. Jupiter bestows great enthusiasm and optimism and provides talents for acting and writing. Such a native becomes a great source to others for inspiration and encouragement and he/she provides a, excellent company to friends. Jupiter in this placement is highly interested in philosophic contemplation, foreign culture and belief system, and travel. Jupiter in this sign grows rapidly and with great zeal. The planet exerts a powerful influence on the native's love life. Jupiter in the 6th house seeks financial and material wealth and is dedicated to achieve these goals. The native tends to do a lot of hard work and possesses a great willpower. Although Jupiter in this placement is generous, it also tends to make the native miser and highly careful to spend his/her earnings. In this placement Jupiter may also cause a devious disposition to benefit the self from others' mistakes and weaknesses. When Jupiter is placed in the 7th house it bestows open-mindedness and makes the individual to find fortune through the people he/she meets. The subject is always open to new ideas and is both impartial and intuitive. As the subject is highly tolerant for different values and lifestyle, he/she is idealistic and humanitarian. Sometimes such natives are also rebellious and easily get bored unless they don't find new avenues in life. Relationship with the partner is based on highly emotional moods. Expectations of the partner are far too high which may result in disruption in relationship with the partner. If the partner does not possess equal intellectual status and education it may also cause disruption in relationship. However, Jupiter's placement in this house is great as far as the individual's personal growth and sustaining persistent belief in spiritual values are concerned as its aspects on the first house are immensely beneficial both financially and spirituality. When Jupiter is placed in the 8th house, financial gain through investment is indicated. Jupiter in this sign bestows emotional depth and provides the native unassuming and friendly disposition. In this placement the native can also be mysterious and withdrawn. It also tends to show a considerable sexual enthusiasm and at times the subject is over-demanding without caring for the partner's needs. Sometimes too much is expected of the partner and so the individual finds satisfaction elsewhere. When Jupiter is placed in the 9th house it provides an independent spirit. The native is highly courageous and possesses a natural talent for leadership. In this placement Jupiter tends to provide an innovative spirit. The subject possesses considerable intellectual potential and his/her outlook on life is very positive. It also affects the subject's imagination positively on account of traveling opportunities, which would broaden the native's vision. The opportunity for higher education is another positive impact of Jupiter's placement in this house besides providing great luck and happiness to the native. When Jupiter is placed in the 10th house it tends to acquire artistic tastes and if Mars is well placed or has its aspects on the fifth house or the ascendant, the native can display his/her interest in architecture, or any other art related fields. In fact, Jupiter in this placement can help the native earn lot of money even through personal business. Its positive aspect on the fourth house is bound to benefit the native from the mother and by 28 years he/she may have good property both mobile and immobile. When Jupiter is placed in the 11th house it tends to offer the subject very adventurous situations that would help him/her grow intellectually, develop social status and provide immense financial benefits. The native may have a large circle of friends, will be very popular, sociable, affluent, and knowledgeable about a wide variety of subjects. Jupiter's direct aspect on the fifth house will benefit the subject with good children who would bring luck to the native. Jupiter's placement in the 12th house may affect the subject's intellectual abilities adversely. It may also mitigate the native's interest in further education and learning, but this placement may bestow optimism and property related benefits. In general, it is going to weaken the intellectual, imaginative as well as logical abilities of the native developing his/her interest in unethical activities. Jupiter in this placement may tend to affect the native with undue emotionalism. When Jupiter is placed in the 1st house (at the ascendant) by far it is one of the best placements in the zodiac system. Not only it bestows courage, self-discipline, determination, honesty, hardworking capacity, religious disposition, but it also makes him/her extremely lucky both financially and materially. The subject may possess good property and able children. Relationship with the children will be positive. He/she will be benefited through long travels and new opportunities provided to him/her on account of Jupiter's aspects on the ninth house. As Jupiter also aspects the seventh house he/she will have a good and a caring partner though he/she may not be so much inclined to the partner emotionally. In this house Jupiter will surely bestow great optimism and enthusiasm, and enhance any talents, especially for acting, painting, writing, leadership and administration. When Jupiter is placed in the 3rd house, it makes the native morally conventional and gives him/her a strong sense of Justice. In this sign Jupiter grows socially. It provides an excellent ability to communicate an unending desire to learn. Jupiter's aspects on the ninth house may bring good luck through long and foreign travels and through jobs where traveling is involved. When Jupiter is placed in the 4th house it provides a strong life-force and makes the subject change jobs a couple of times. This placement is good for the mother's health, relationship with the parents and to possess a good residence. So far we have discussed Jupiter's placement in different houses when it owns the fifth house in Sagittarius. Let us now consider its transits in different houses when it owns the sign Pisces in the fifth house.

When Jupiter transits in Pisces and owns the fifth house it will bestow almost similar results what it would do when it owns the fifth house in Sagittarius except that its placement in the 7th, 12th, and the 3rd houses may not be as fruitful. In the 7th house it may constantly disturb the relationship with the partner on account of lack understanding and different approaches to life; when placed in the 12th house it may make the native extravagant, fruitless wanderer, less social and unreliable; when it is placed in the third house it may make the subject less effortful, schemer and not sailing smoothly with brothers and friends, but it exalted aspects on the ninth house is surely going to provide good luck to the subject by offering him/her great opportunities through travel related jobs, private business or as an astrologer or writer. When Jupiter owns the fifth house and sits in the ninth house or ascendant, this placement by and large is considered to be very good as it bestows great luck through long travels, including traveling for religious purposes, elevates social status, brings affluence of every kind, provides leadership qualities, and offers great job opportunities.

Transits of Venus

Venus is mainly associated with things desirable and admirable such as love, beauty and love of beauty, admiration of arts, peace and reconciliation, harmony, enjoyment of pleasure and feminine nature in women and men as well. Astrologers consider that planet's influence can be felt in all kind of relationships such as social ties, business, love and sexual bonds. If Venus is placed favorably in a chart it tends to make the individual gentle, warm-hearted, sentimental, graceful and artistic. But if it is weak or negatively placed it makes an individual lazy, indecisive, excessively romantic, un-pragmatic, careless, envious and jealous. Venus rules two signs, Taurus and Libra and corresponds to kidneys and throat in human body including physical beauty.

When Venus transits in Taurus and owns the fifth house the native is always steadfast and takes time in cultivating romance. The subject often becomes very possessive about them whom he/she loves. Such a native possesses a great aesthetic sense which manifests itself in comely surroundings. The subject is always charming, sensual, artistic, and committed in his/her disposition. The native has an attractive personality as such easily fascinates others. The subject takes great pleasure in creative work and has a great liking for acting, writing, painting, and all types of artistic pursuits. If Venus has good aspects from friendly planets, this placement may bring benefits through investments and even speculations. In this placement Venus also offers great opportunities in teaching job, art and stage related jobs, cinema-script writer, acting and pleasure seeking areas. When Venus is placed in the 6th house it may bestow good human relationship on the job. This placement is good for counselors, arbitrators, health-care workers, jobs associated with artistic pursuits, and media. Such natives may have high social connections and possess great communicative qualities, leading to over indulgence at times. When Venus is placed in the 7th house the subject is often romantic and sensitive. The native is likely to rush into anything without giving much thought to it. The subject is highly emotional and tends to cultivate good and sensuous relationship with the partner. The seventh house should always be interpreted together with the fifth house (the house of creativity and love) which indicates the subject's attitude towards the act of love and having children. In this placement the individual is socially very active and commands good friends who stand by him/her when need arises. This placement helps to deal with the public and works well in sales, or as a psychologist, performing arts and public relations. When Venus is placed in the 8th house the native is loyal and faithful. He/she prefers a very comfortable life and is driven to earn good deal of money. The subject loves fine things and when in love he/she is too much in love with those things. Venus in this placement creates a passionate love towards the partner. The native looks for and finds sexual fulfillment and often inherits money or property from a loved one. In this placement Venus bestows intense emotions and possessiveness. When Venus is placed in the 9th house, it tends to make the native gentle, modest, unassuming and charming. At times the individual may possess a tendency to over criticize others, but this placement makes him/her very effortful, highly communicative, and caring for art, acting, and stage- related jobs. Venus in this placement also cares for high ideals and appreciation for different cultures. This placement also indicates that the native may marry a foreigner and spend much of his/her life abroad. When Venus is placed in the 10th house, it indicates careers in arts or cultural work. The native enjoys social success and prosperity from art- related jobs. The individual is very natural at diplomacy and possesses ability to use one's social charisma to achieve success in public service. In this placement Venus may provide jobs in counselling, diplomatic relations, judiciary and acting in films areas. In fact, it is a very positive placement of Venus, which brings social status, money, fame and financial benefits, but he/she may not have many friends or brothers. When Venus is placed in the 11th house, it helps the native to have good friends and to be associated with people, both socially and financially. In this placement Venus indicates an idealistic disposition and develops interest in ethical values. The planet helps to cultivate musical talents and artistic qualities in this placement. Such natives make excellent teamplayers. Its aspect on the fifth house indicates more number of daughters, a very sensuous disposition and the native is highly sexually inclined, very emotional and imaginative. When Venus is placed in the 12th house, it tends to make the subject compassionate and sympathetic. However, in this placement Venus is not quite favourable for job opportunities nor it helps in enriching native's imagination. However, this placement tends to make the native highly critical against others, make him/her spendthrift indulging in unsocial activities influencing adversely his/her social status. As worldly success is less in sight, the subject turns to God and devotes a lot of time in worshiping and praying although such pursuits may not be quite genuine. The individual is also noted for secretive love affairs and personal contacts but quite conspicuous in artistic pursuits.

When Venus is placed in the 1st house, it is a very positive placement to provide social status and a highly motivated personality towards acting and art- related jobs. The subject has a gifted imagination and very compassionate disposition. The individual is emotionally and loyally inclined towards the partner, rich financially and is often associated with jobs related to judiciary and amusement. When Venus is placed in the 2nd house, it tends to make the native diplomatic and excelling in the art of a balanced speech. He/she is often emotionally detached and original in his/ her love pursuits. In this placement Venus cares a great deal about freedom and openness. Such a native is often cool, calm, collected and detached. When Venus is placed in the 3rd house, it makes the native extremely effortful and successful in different errands and projects. The subject possesses a very fascinating personality, always eager to pursue his/her goals with great zeal and force. The native is often highly imaginative and creative especially in writing, acting, music and administration. He/she is often associated with finance- related jobs, socially very wellplaced and financially affluent. When Venus is placed in the 4th house, it may make the native selfish, very agile and quick in making love, often frustrated, less imaginative, but gets good job opportunities, and cultivates uneven relationship with the parents, especially with the mother. The subject is not attached to home, often arrogant and less inclined to further learning. So far we have discussed Venus's transits in different houses when it owns the fifth house in Taurus. We shall discuss now its placement in Libra in the fifth house.

When Venus transits in Libra in the fifth house and moves to different houses, it is bound to give similar results what it would provide when rising in Taurus in the fifth house it transits in various houses, except that in the 7th, 12th, and 4th houses it may not be much beneficial. In the 7th house it may tend the native flirting with the opposite sex and may spend a lot of money to fulfil his/her sex desires. The native loves freedom, as such he/she may not be trust worthy as far as relationship with the partner is concerned. In fact, Venus in this placement bestows an *expensive* love. But its aspects on the ascendant make the individual highly vocal and richly communicative. When placed in the 12th house it may mitigate the subject's imaginative capabilities, may cause loss to some of his/her children; the subject's interest in learning will be mitigated but he/she may be interested in music and spend a lot of money un-fruitfully in travelling. When Venus is placed in the 4th house, it may lead to uneven relationship with the mother, and motivate the native to change his/her residence several times until the subject has reached the age of 52 years. But in this placement Venus may provide the subject to have several good job opportunities, especially in the fields of art, culture or acting. However, its placement in the 8th, 9th and 10th houses will highly be rewarding. In the 8th it tends to provide a lot of lifeforce and creativity. The subject's sex life will be quite fascinating and he/she will have a lot of attachment towards the partner making life happier. In the 9th house it will bring great luck through children and through the company of some influential friends and well-settled brothers. Both in the 9th and 10th houses its placement may provide great job opportunities in art and amusement- related areas and may give the individual high positions in revenue and finance- related departments. It may help cultivating great imagination and creativity, especially in the fields associated with writing, acting, music and stage direction. When Venus is placed in the 1st house, it provides intellectual stimulation and the subject's life is full of romance. He/she is highly communicative and will possess love of language. It also provides a great social status and a deep desire to keep the company of opposite sex. Venus in the 3rd house may make the native speak less with caution. The native will highly be effortful though will receive less positive yields. In this placement the individual is often static in his/her disposition and may be noted for his single-mindedness.

Transits of Saturn

Saturn is the second largest planet after Jupiter. Saturn represents responsibility and authority. It also represents internal authority or conscience and self-control. Saturn's influence can inspire or destroy. When it is placed positively in a chart it will bestow managerial capability, persistence, endurance, prudence, carefulness in money matters, and right mindfulness. When Saturn is placed positively in a chart, it is bound to make a native love careers in the government, military, business, religion and jobs related to philosophical pursuits; but if negatively placed, it may tend to develop cruelty, selfishness, deviousness and self-indulgence in the native. In fact, Saturn represents one's ambitious side and so it is well aware of one's strengths and weaknesses. Saturn's orbit of the Sun takes twentynine- and- a -half years to complete its full circle. It rules body's aging process and creates rheumatism, hardening of arteries and degeneration of organs. Saturn rules Capricorn and Aquarius. (Cosmic connections, p. 44) Let us discover Saturn's impact on an individual when it transits in Capricorn and in Aquarius in the fifth house and other houses being the owner of the fifth house.

When Saturn transits in Capricorn in the fifth house, it makes the native ambitious and persistent. The individual intends to succeed. In this placement Saturn makes the subject disciplined and hardworking but at times it also makes him/her heard-hearted. Fifth house Saturn makes an individual over disciplined, therefore, the native needs to learn how to relax and have a good time. Because of its seriousness Saturn's placement in the fifth house leads to creativity, mostly in the field of science, but the fields of art and music cannot be overruled. The native with this placement loves to work in business associated with investments, speculation, education, places of entertainment and in arts. It also, at times, manifests as ambition for leadership or to possess positions in artistic fields, or working in printing and publishing areas. Such a subject is often romantically attracted to someone who is older or more matured in feelings. The subject may also be blessed with four or five sons who will be fairly wellplaced in life. Since Saturn aspects the 7th, 11th and the 2nd houses in the chart. As such, it may create problems to his/her family and married life, will help to earn money by hard work and honest means and may provide the ability of good conversation. When Saturn is placed in the 6th house, it is often humanitarian, reliable, innovative, and possesses the ability to know the self. Such a native wants both freedom and discipline. The individual is often personal, detached and ready to express one's own views different from others. As a result, it causes to reduce the number of close friends. In this placement Saturn tends to make the native work hard with great attention. Its aspects on the 8th house may provide the subject a long and healthy life, get money from a near relative and give him/her invariable self-confidence. But its aspects on the 3rd house may bestow upon the native a lazy attitude towards work and mitigate relationship with friends. When Saturn is placed in the 7th house, the subject is often hesitant to form an emotional relationship with the partner but if once it is formed he/she is extremely faithful. It has been observed that Saturn in this placement causes association with a partner senior to the native. This placement may also delay marriages and lead to separation or create constant disturbance to one's married life, unless there are good aspects on the seventh house. This is a good placement for working in legal system or business management. From this placement Saturn aspects the ninth, first and the fourth houses. Its aspects on the ninth and the first houses are extremely beneficial and will gradually bestow good luck, fortune, financial affluence and social status, but its aspects on the fourth house may not be as lucrative and may tend to change one's residence quite often, jeopardize the mother's health and lead to changing jobs. When Saturn is placed in the 8th house, it indicates sexual shyness or inhibition of some kind. The subject is unable to express one's emotions openly. In this placement Saturn usually bestows a long life and gets financial support from one's close relatives. Such an individual needs to learn independence, self-reliance and patience, as Saturn is in its debilitated sign. From the eighth house Saturn aspects the tenth, second and the fifth houses. All these aspects are highly beneficial to the native in providing great job opportunities, good speech habits, cultivating right imagination and longing to get higher education. When Saturn is placed in the 9th house, this again is a very beneficial placement. Being the owner of the fifth sitting in the house of luck and creativity, it tends to enhance native's luck, financial and social status, making the subject highly productive in the fields of art or science. The subject tends to be a great innovator and humanitarian and leans towards spirituality, philosophy and religion. It is also observed that in this placement Saturn may induce an inherent distrust of new ideas, because it is interested in social stability and provides great wisdom as the native advances in age. In the ninth house Saturn often makes the individual to seek positions of authority in the fields of religious institutions, education or businesses related with law, politics, international affairs, publishing, media, or get high positions in diplomatic fields, military or similar departments.

When Saturn is placed in the 10th house, it provides a great ability of problem-solving and a deep desire for life- long learning. Saturn in this placement also indicates discipline, natural intelligence and patience to succeed on to the goal. The individual possesses a strong drive to succeed and is determined to remove all the obstacles on the path of success. As Saturn creates a desire and need to be responsible, the native often excels in business and politics. When Saturn is strong in degrees in this house or has beneficial aspects, it tends to provide positions of authority and high salaries. However, Saturn, in this placement, may also inspire the individual to deviate from values, which may be detrimental to retain the high positions for long. It is, therefore, necessary for the subject to learn to stick to values and abandon personal interests. As Saturn aspects, twelfth, fourth and the seventh houses, it may make the native spendthrift, inspire to change the residence and develop uneven relationship with the partner. When Saturn is placed in the 11th house, it indicates problems in early childhood. The native is not free to act and needs approval and security from others. Saturn also tends to create in the native constant worry and withdrawal tendency that affects the relationship with the partner. There is some kind of internal fear in the subject that checks him/her to act freely. It results in the disruption of the relationship with the partner. But in this placement Saturn helps in building a good social status and having a few strong and meaningful friends. The planet develops great organizational ability in the native. Its aspects on the fifth house helps the children to grow successfully and its aspects on the first house make him/her highly productive, creative and imaginative. From this placement the planet also aspects the eighth house which brings financial gains and long life. When Saturn is placed in the 12th house, the native is extremely self-assured, often pompous and not straightforward as far as close conversations are concerned. Such a native strongly desires to reach the position of recognition and importance, because he/she is highly egoistic. Because of a predominant ego the subject's values are distorted or twisted in his/her own advantage. Saturn placed in the 12th house often makes the native reserved, lonely and afraid. He/she is quite secretive and doesn't share personal feelings with others. The individual possesses unfounded fears either imaginary or associated with the subject's past memories.

Its aspects on the 2nd, 6th and the 9th houses provide mixed results. As a result, the native is very cautious in his/her speech, earns money with hard work, and likes to work in large companies, institutions run by the government. Such natives often find work in big forms as clerks or cashiers too.

When Saturn is placed in the 1st house, it is a very positive placement and helps the native to rise from low positions to a very high level. In this placement Saturn is one step ahead of its exaltation sign, as such, after the age of 48 years the individual gets excellent job or promotional opportunities. Money wise the subject is greatly benefited and his/her social status also gets promoted. He/she commands a very high position in law or judiciary departments, as Saturn aspects the tenth house. Saturn also aspects the third house, so it makes the native quite effortful and productive, and gets him/her complete benefit of the intellectual abilities. The subject is self-disciplined and wellorganized. He/she is very serious and hardworking. Such a native commands high imaginative ability with which he/she is able to complete the well-planned projects. As his/her productivity is great his/her social status is also immense. A first house Saturn bestows sensibility and orderliness on the natives, which make them very successful. But this placement is detrimental for the relationship with the partner. The planet somehow in some way builds suspicion, which mars the relationship between the native and the partner. When Saturn is placed in the 2nd house, it is highly beneficial for higher learning and may provide opportunities to go abroad for studies. Saturn formulates high ambitions that inspire the native to make long-range financial planning leading to material comforts and financial affluence. Saturn makes the subject work hard to achieve financial security. The subject is shrewd and cautious. The gains may be slow but surely they will be steady. In this placement Saturn might create worry about money, even if the native doesn't need it. He/she can do very well with realestate, investments, government and business contracts, management and construction. The native will do well in any other work made for the long-rage gains. In fact, in this placement Saturn provides a great sense of responsibility and honesty, which work good to build relationship with others. The subject is benefited with a great insight for a fair judgment and achieves great success in public life. He/she knows the need to establish long and lasting relationships with others to build anything of long-term value and friendship. In this placement the planet also bestows long and healthy life if the ascendant is also wellplaced in the chart. When Saturn is placed in the 3rd house, it makes the subject serious, capable, resourceful and full of insight. The planet induces a deep desire to learn things in order to put them to good use. In this placement Saturn provides practical aptitude that makes the individual strong in scientific and mathematical ability. Such a native might work in publishing, as a researcher, a librarian, an accountant, in media or communication department, a teacher, and might get opportunity to go abroad to join cultural groups to participate in cultural festivals. Saturn's placement in the 4th house may provide early disappointments in life and drawbacks in education. It may also be detrimental for the health of the mother and take the subject away from the native place towards the West. But as the individual grows older, he/she learns wisdom and becomes more successful both in learning and material gains. In this placement Saturn may incur early loss of one of the parents—possibly loss of father. Therefore, the planet makes the subject gradually learn how to plan for the future and to take care of the family and traditions. Saturn's aspects on the tenth and first houses are of immense benefit providing the native good job opportunities, though somewhat late, and inducing insight to see things in advance. The native might also be secretive and would not reveal the inner self easily as the planet's aspects on the first house makes him/her quite prudent.

When Saturn is transiting in Aquarius in the fifth house, it will provide similar results what it would give when transiting in Capricorn in the fifth house except that its transits or impact on the 7th, 11th, 2nd houses will not be beneficial. When transiting the 7th house, it will create problems to one's married life, failures in love affairs and ill health to the mother or loss of father, but will give a good social status, provide wisdom and lead to successful career in the later period of life, making the subject financially affluent. When placed in the 11th house, it may mitigate social status, reduce the number of trusted friends, and result in the loss of children as well as romantic pursuits. It may further incur failure in business leading to financial losses. When transiting the 2nd house it may bestow an unpleasant speech style that would incur dislike and unpleasantness of others. It may also lead to financial losses as projects will fail and would not be completed. But this placement may extend the lifespan of the native and provide quite a satisfactory sex life. Its placement in the 10th house may also not be quite beneficial as far as job opportunities and married life are concerned except that if the Moon is wellplaced and Jupiter has favorable aspects on the seventh and tenth the subject may not experience adverse effects on those counts. Saturn's placement in the 5th as well as in the 1st house will highly be beneficial giving the native a good number of able children, great status in the society, great job opportunities in revenue, military, engineering departments, or opportunities in film industry or any business associated with stage, entertainment or amusement areas. In rest of houses Saturn should provide similar results what it would give when placed in the fifth house in Capricorn.

So far we have been discussing Saturn's transits in Capricorn and Aquarius when placed in the fifth as well as owning the fifth house. Let us now discuss certain rules or principles that we may deduce from Saturn's transits in different houses when owning the 5th house before we analyze charts (*kundalis*) for the benefit of the reader.

The Rules

1. ***The fifth house is associated with children, creativity, and romance. As such, when a planet sits in its own sign in the fifth house, or aspects it from any position, it would provide good and favourable results. Thus, it would give able children, fill the subject's life with romance and make him/her creative in a field associated***

or influenced by the owners of the fifth house and the ascendant, or the owners of the 9th and 10th houses.

2. ***Owner of the 5th house must bestow highly beneficial results in its own sign or in a friendly or exalted sign when placed in the 1st, 9th, 10th, or 11th houses irrespective of the placement of its other sign transiting in a less beneficial house.***
3. ***Different planets, relating to children, romance or creativity, will produce variable results when placed in their own signs in the fifth house.***

For example, if Mars is the owner of the fifth, it may give only one or two sons, provide an aggressive romantic life and make the native creative in the field of science. When Venus is the owner of the fifth house, the native may possess more number of daughters, may excel in acting, arts, music, painting and cultural fields and possess a highly sensuous and romantic disposition. When Jupiter is the owner of the fifth, it may give a couple of highly cultivated children, the native will like to keep the company of intellectual and an educated partner or highly cultured women, and will show his/her creativity in writing, publishing, producing spirituality related literature. When Mercury is the owner of the fifth, it may give very active and educated children, the native will be good in writing and publishing, and keep the company of educated women or have a spouse who has a lot of understanding and consideration. When Saturn is the owner of the fifth house, it may make the subject fall in love with someone who would be senior in age or matured in feelings, provide four or five wellplaced sons, and make the native produce literature in the fields of philosophy, science, religion, spirituality or related to another world. When the Sun is the owner of the fifth house, it will provide a couple of wellplaced children, the native may tend to fall in romance very rapidly, and will be productive as an administrator and possess unparalleled leadership qualities. When the Moon is the owner of the fifth, it may give more number of daughters, make the native highly imaginative and provide poetic talents, and will be highly romantic in nature.

All this is a broad but pointed discussion about the owner of the fifth house sitting in the fifth house. But these results can be accelerated or mitigated when the owner of the fifth house has aspects from the beneficial or friendly planets. If the fifth house has aspects from the unfriendly planets (like Jupiter being the owner and has aspects from Venus), the benefits will be lessened or take a different direction. It can be better understood with the help of examples or when the interested reader goes on analyzing charts for years, many such matters will easily be understood by him/her. Let us analyze a number of charts to clarify/justify the rules stated here above.

Example 1

Following is the chart of the native currently working as a homoeopathic doctor.

Native born on 17th June, 1979

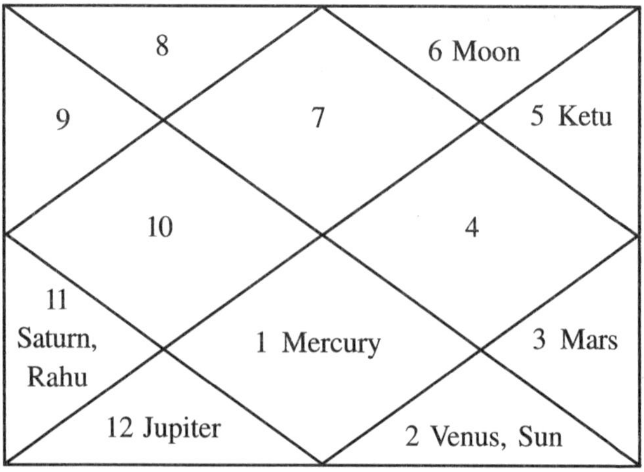

Discussions

The native was born in one of the Southern States of the country and was raised in a considerably moderate family. Early family problems did not let the native go for very high education yet the subject having a deep desire to do something started acquiring knowledge about homoeopathy. The native's ascendant Venus placed with the Sun in the 8th house gets a energy and life-force that would always keep the individual agile and ready to work for others. The Moon, owner of the 10th sitting in the 12th house, suggests a private job. Mars's aspect on the Moon indicates that the native will have a leaning towards medical science. *Above all it is the placement of Saturn in Aquarius in the fifth house, which provides a great quality of work and desire to create something new and progressive. As such, the native will always try to go deeper into the causes of human ailment and like to find out the best ways to treat the people so that they get redeemed soon.* It is expected that the subject will gradually enjoy the benefits of the job and will be recognized as a good homoeopathic doctor, in spite of the fact that there may be early financial problems. Jupiter's exalted aspect on the tenth house is likely to get a good placement (job) and high reputation to the native.

Example 2

The following chart belongs to a promising student pursuing undergraduate courses in science.

Native born on 18th June, 1985

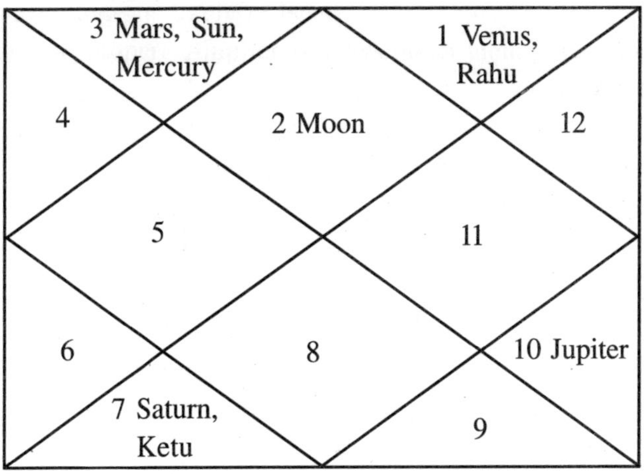

Discussions

The owner of the 5th house Mercury is sitting in its own sign in the second house, which happens to be the tenth house from the fifth. As such, the native is bound to be very productive. There is much likelihood that he would go for research in the field of science. Besides, the owner of the ninth, Saturn responsible for higher education, is sitting in the 6th house in its exalted position. Therefore, it is quite positive that the native will complete his Ph. D. degree in a near future. It is also possible that the subject may excel in computer science and will earn lot of money through that business. Since Mercury is conjunct with the Sun it is also a great possibility that the native would excel in mathematics and related field. Mercury is also conjunct with Mars, which also gives indication that the native may study subjects related to engineering and computer. The native's chart contains an exalted Moon on the ascendant, which is really good for friendship and social relationship. But his ascendant Venus is sitting in the twelfth house, which indicates waste of efforts and time and, consequently, affects his achievements adversely.

One must keep in view that like the owner of the ninth, the owner of the fifth house would also bring good results when it occupies a good house and a good sign. The good effects of a planet would increase when it is conjunct with beneficial (yogakarak) planets. For example, Mercury conjunct with the Sun becomes highly beneficial for the study of mathematics and science, including computer science. Besides, when the owner of the ninth is in its exalted position and is sitting in the tenth house from its ownership, it will certainly help the native attain higher education.

Example 3

The following chart belongs to a lady lecturer who is working in the Department of Education in a progressive Deemed to be University in one of the southern states of the country.

Native born on 20th March, 1957

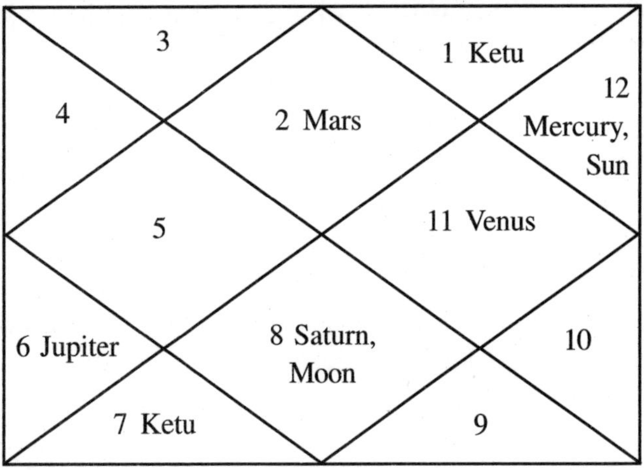

Discussions

The above chart indicates an exchange of the owners of the fifth and the eleventh houses. It clearly reflects earnings through teaching or education. Although debilitated Mercury, owner of the 5th house, is sitting in the 7th house from its lordship, it has its exalted aspects on the fifth house. As such, the native has completed Ph.D. in Education although Mercury is combust with the Sun. There is one more factor to help her complete her higher education. The owner of the ninth, Saturn sitting in the 7th house has aspects on the ninth house. It has not only helped her to attain further education, but it is also going to give her opportunities for foreign travel as well. When this chart is being analyzed (December, 2005), the native has already attained 48 years of age. She will have opportunity to travel abroad within one-and-a-half year as well as after eight years from the time of the analysis of this chart.

A careful examination of the 5th house reveals that the native's basic education and insight is slightly mitigated as the owner of the fifth Mercury is sitting in its debilitated sign and is also combust with the Sun. However, Jupiter sitting in the fifth being the owner of the 11th house has increased the possibility of being rich in experience in her own field as well as rich financially and socially. There is another good yoga, which is formed by the placement of the ascendant in the 10th from its own position. It has increased the job opportunities and benefits, and provided her an artistic bent of mind. The subject may do well if she keeps on doing writing work or is involved with media or broadcasting agencies.

Example 4

The following chart belongs to a Professor of Chemistry working in an established University of the country.

Native born on 15th May, 1956

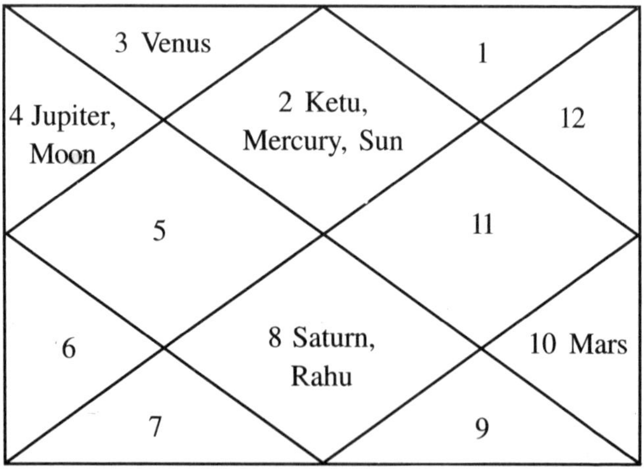

Discussions

There is an exchange between the owners of the ascendant and the second house. It clearly indicates that the native is not only vocally strong but is also quite productive as the owner of the fifth Mercury, is sitting at the ascendant. The native's chart has Mars and Jupiter in their exalted positions. It has increased the status of the chart in the sense that the native is highly effortful, influential and has great political and social connections.

Though in this section of the book we are limiting our discussion to the fifth house only, the native's owner of the ninth house, Saturn, is very strong and has aspects from its owner too. It indicates foreign travels and benefits from such journeys. But Saturn's aspect on the ascendant, especially on the Sun, is not beneficial. It indicates less achievement property-wise and also indicates transfer of residence towards the south or west from his native place.

Well, considering the strength of the owner of the fifth house, it can be predicted that the native is quite productive in his field and will have a good number of successful Ph.D. scholars to his credit, including completing a good number of research projects. The owner of the fifth Mercury sitting at the ascendant tends to create romantic and artistic feelings in the native and provides him with the writing ability which would bring him great name and honour in life.

Example 5

The following chart belongs to a secondary school student who is playing Tennis at the International level as an Indian representative at such an early stage.

Native born on 28th December, 1990

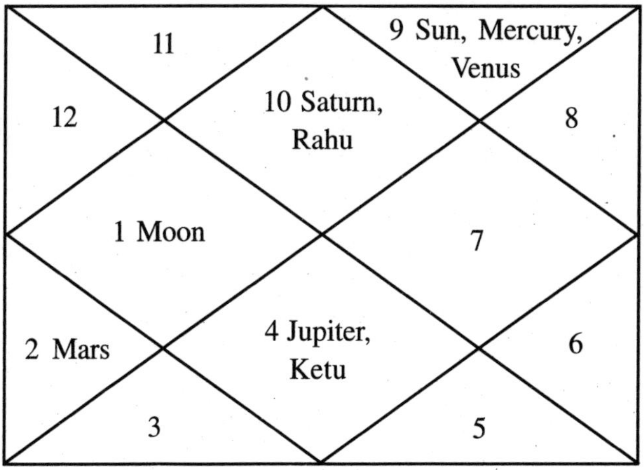

Discussions

The native is hardly sixteen years old but he has been excelling in Tennis representing his country at the international level a couple of times at this age. Mars, the owner of the 11th (gains & social status) is sitting in the fifth house which is related with sports, romance, productivity and children. The reader must keep in view that aspects play a great role in astrology in providing benefits or losses. As such, Mars's aspects on the 8th house and on its owner, Sun as well, also indicate great life-force that has provided tremendous energy to the native with which he persistently fights his opponents to win the matches. The owner of the fifth Venus is also the ruler of the 10th and is sitting with the owner of the 9th Mercury. Well, it indicates some loss of efforts on the part of the native. But as the Sun is sitting with those two planets, they are revitalized by it. Let the reader must not forget that the eighth house owner sitting anywhere is going to provide energy and strength to the house as well as the planets with which it sits. Thus, the owner of the fifth house, Venus, in spite of being combust, also gets strength, as it is conjunct with the Sun. But it also creates other possibilities. The native is likely to get jobs in private establishments only and may change a number of jobs before finally settling down.

Let us keep in view the chart of the Cricket wizard has also such combinations. His chart has been discussed once again in this book at an appropriate place. In his case an exalted Mars sitting in the fifth house, aspects the exalted Sun sitting in the eighth house. Though the position of the planets in the above chart are not exactly the same but to some extent they are quite identical as Mars sitting in the fifth house aspects the eighth house which is ruled by the Sun. In fact, the eighth house in the above referred chart has become very strong as its owner Sun is sitting in the 12th house creating Vipreet Raj Yoga.*

---

*Please read about Vipreet Raj Yoga in our book—**Explore the Power of Astrology.**

Example 6

The following chart belongs to a senior lecturer in Public Administration who is working at one of the established University in southern India.

Native born on 31st July, 1963

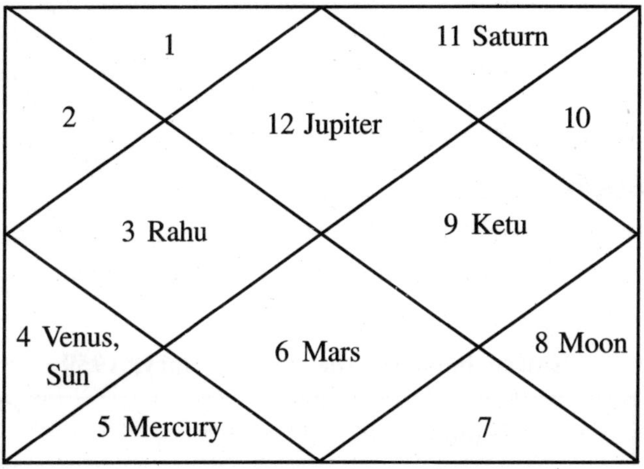

Discussions

The owner of the fifth house Moon is sitting in the ninth house which has become highly beneficial (*yoga kara*) being fifth from the fifth. As such, it makes the native highly productive, emotional and full of rage at times. It also creates a likelihood that the native will be indulged in writing work after the 33 years of his age but quite extensively after 44 years of his age.

In fact, it is a very good example of a chart in which the fifth house is very strong. The owner of the ascendant Jupiter, which is in its own house and is also the owner of the 10th, aspects the fifth (with an exalted look) as well as the ninth house where Moon is sitting. It helps the native to get good and productive children (both a male and female), and provides him opportunities to do good research work. It also indicates that he will get some very productive and agile research scholars, who will successfully pass-out under his guidance.

As we are limiting our discussion on the 5th house in this section, we would like to draw the attention of the reader to observe how strong is the 5th house in the above chart, though its owner, Moon, is in its debilitated sign. The owner of the fifth sitting in the ninth has become very strong and will bring the native benefits from his children and partner and from his research scholars as well. It may also make him highly emotional and create a leaning to be more talkative as well.

Example 7

The following chart belongs to a Medical Jurist who is working as a Reader in a Medical College in a Northern University in the country.

Native born on the 4th February, 1959

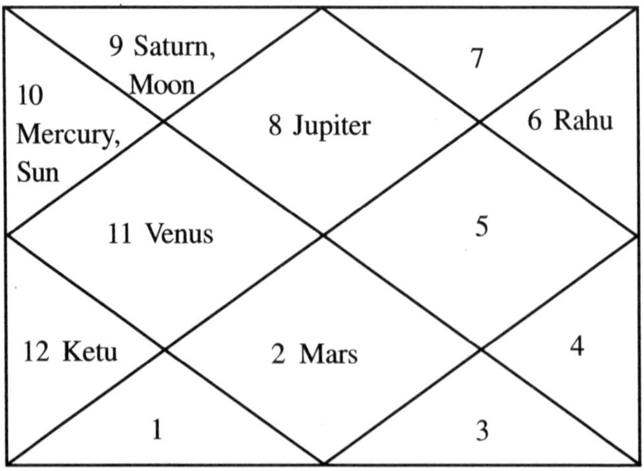

Discussions

The above chart is another good example of a productive 5th house as its owner Jupiter is sitting at the ascendant. Though Ketu sitting in the 5th has mitigated some benefits relating to the fifth house, Jupiter as *yoga kara* has restored its benefits to the native, providing him a unique kind of agility and strength towards studies and research. It gives him the benefits of having two progressive children and makes in him a leaning to invest his efforts in new dimensions. Besides completing his MS in the field of medical jurist, he has also attained a degree in Law, which has, in fact, no direct relationship with the medical field (except that it is beneficial in medical jurist field). The doctor is also keenly indulged with Homoeopathy and is keenly interested in astrology mainly related to the criminal field. *The 5th house is mainly concerned with children, romance, productivity and sports.* In the doctor's case, except indulging in sports, the fifth house has benefited him with good children and a romantic married life as the partner is highly devoted (Venus sitting in a beneficial sign and house as well). It has made him highly productive and expert in his field, which has bestowed upon him early promotions in the job. Let us not forget the good aspects of the fifth on the ninth house. Jupiter being the owner of the fifth has its exalted aspect on the ninth house. This itself is a very good yoga though the owner of the ninth, Moon, is conjunct with Saturn in the 2nd house.

Example 8

The following chart belongs to a professor of Chemistry working in an established University in the country.

Native born on 24th February, 1956

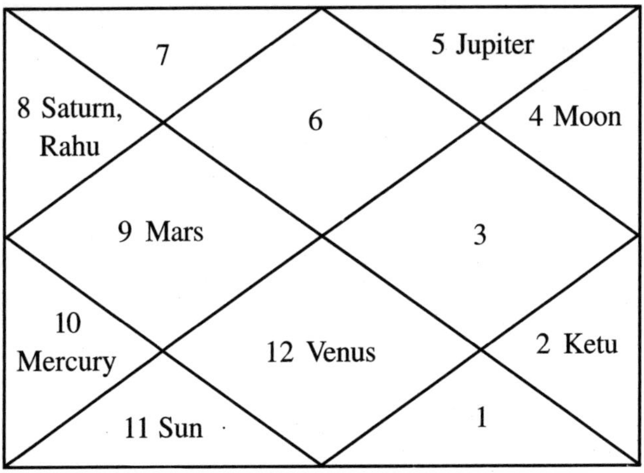

Discussions

It is one of the best examples of a highly beneficial and productive 5th house as the owner of the ascendant Mercury, a natural friend of Saturn and owner of the 5th, is sitting in the 5th house. It has helped the native in boosting the quality of eloquence, increasing his capacity of productivity and benefited him with highly promising children. There is another positive yoga in the chart as far as the 5th house is concerned. The owner of the 5th Saturn not only aspects the 5th house from the 3rd, it also has a beneficial aspect on the 9th house. Consequently, it benefits him with the promising children, good luck, and a good a caring partner, as well as it helps him produce good written material, such as, books and articles that would bestow upon him respect from his colleagues and people at large. The material that the professor has produced so far is quite conspicuous to identify him as an imaginative writer. Since an exalted Venus owner of the 9th is sitting in the 11th house from its position, it is going to provide him good luck and financial benefits, although it has its debilitated aspect on the ascendant.

The reader must keep in view a great beneficial interchange of aspects between Mercury and a strong Moon that bestows upon him great insight and emotional fervour to produce some distinguished written material as highly beneficial Mercury provides him the quality of communication both in writing and speech.

Example 9

The following chart belongs to a lady lecturer in Geology in a Government College in a Western State of the country.

Native born on 22nd June, 1965

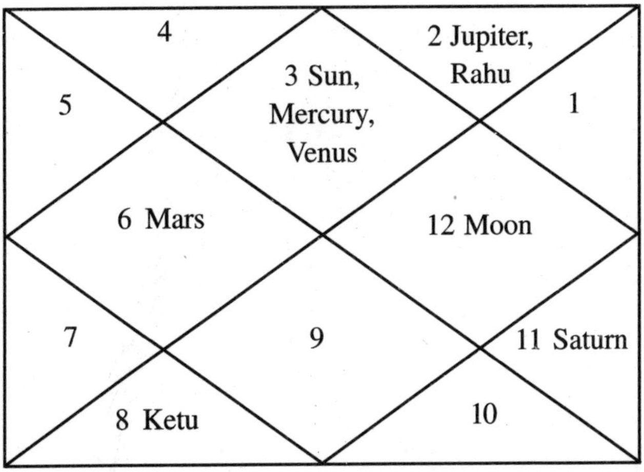

Discussions

The above chart is another good example of a powerful fifth house, as its owner Venus is sitting at the ascendant with its natural friend Mercury and the owner of the 3rd house Sun. It bestows upon the native a charming personality, having the quality of a powerful speech, implicit with good and charming diction.

Although the owner of the tenth house, Jupiter, is sitting in the 12th house, the native is still working in a Government College as her ascendant Mercury is conjunct with Venus and has restored the most of the lost opportunities. Jupiter's placement in the 12th house as the owner of the 7th also indicates some problems with his partner, but as she will have good and caring children and, therefore, that dismal part of her life will get fulfilled through her promising and able children. A strong and a wellplaced Venus also indicates the lady's interest in music, art, culture and literature. When her chart is being analyzed (December 2005) she has attained almost forty years of age. It is very much likely that her 45th year will highly be productive, lucky and may give her opportunity to travel abroad or to travel far and distant lands as a strong Saturn, which is the owner of the ninth, is sitting in its own house.

Example 10

The following chart belongs to a professional engineer but currently working as a housewife.

Native born on 24th November, 1976

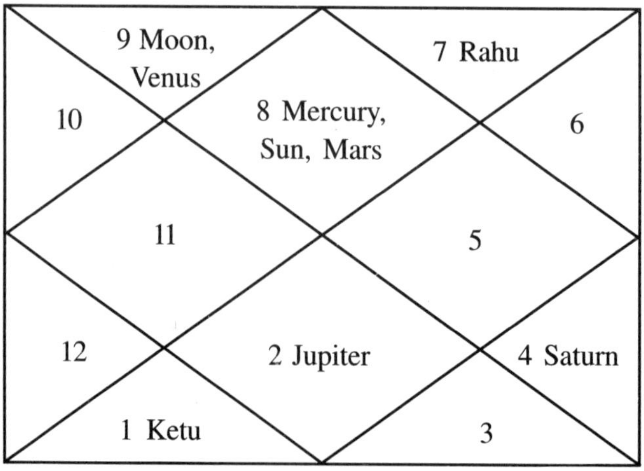

Discussions

We are presenting a unique chart for the advantage of the readers to show that even though the native's ascendant and the owner of the 10th house are very strong, the native had to leave the job on account of her marriage. There is an exchange of the 2nd and the 7th house owners—Venus and Jupiter. Jupiter is also the ruler of the 5th house. As such, the exchange between the two natural enemies has adversely affected the outcome of the 5th house, and, to some extent, Venus sitting in the enemy's house has mitigated her luck in respect of her partner as her partner is less equipped educationally and professionally as she is. Besides, the only child she has is not totally very normal in the sense he/she is almost four years old, yet his/her does not possess normal speech. As such, the voice of the child and his body functions are not absolutely normal. The owner of the 5th Jupiter sitting in the 7th house in its enemy's sign has disrupted both the child normality, as well as her husband's position.

The reader, therefore, must keep in mind that a planet can be good or bad in view of its ownership, placement and the sign it occupies. Both Jupiter and Venus sitting in their enemys' house/sign have disturbed the fifth and the seventh houses in their own way. The native had to leave her job on account of her partner and a child that would take birth later on. She has an engineering degree that she passed out in good grades. Immediately after graduation she got a good job in a reputed Company, where she worked for almost four years after her marriage, but she had to relinquish her job after marriage. Her ascendant and the owners of the tenth and eleventh houses—Mars, Sun and Mercury—are conjunct at the ascendant. Therefore, though she left the job, she has started teaching senior class students at home and has begun earning quite a good amount of money each month. Thus, the good ascendant and the owners of the tenth and eleventh have not let her remain idle, and helped her earn money to support her family even when she is without a formal job.

Example 11

The following chart belongs to a Research Scholar in Chemistry, whose engagement took place in the second week of December 2005.

Native born on 23rd November, 1980

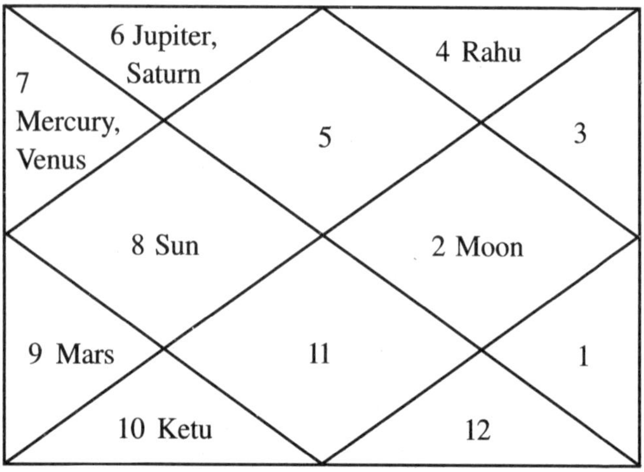

Discussions

The above chart is another good example of a wellplaced owner of the fifth house. It has brought good luck to the native at the age of 24 years plus as far as her marriage is concerned. When this analysis is being made, Jupiter is transiting in the 3rd house of the native and has direct aspect on the ninth house, which is the house of its natural friend, Mars. The native has almost completed her Ph.D. in Chemistry, and is being benefited by taking senior classes in a University wherefrom she is completing her research project.

Therefore, one must keep in mind the role of the fifth house, which provides benefits in view of its placement in a good and beneficial house. Its placement in the tenth house from its ownership has helped the native to complete her research project well in time. When this analysis is being done Jupiter is transiting in the sign Libra. From that position

it looks not only at the seventh house but also at the ninth house. It has provided opportunities to get engaged at the age of 24 years. It has also provides her opportunities to go abroad in a very near future as her would-be partner has been working abroad. The owner of the ninth also aspects the 8th house, which provides the native great lifeforce, energy and courage. As we are only concentrating on the fifth house and its lordship in this section, we are not analyzing the effects of Saturn on the Sun, which is the ascendant of the native. In fact, such aspects do bring some kind of doggedness in the native's character and may bring some personal problems on account of the Sun (ascendant) having aspects from its natural enemy Saturn. However, the owners of the tenth and the eleventh have aspects on the ninth house, which is highly beneficial in terms of good luck, job opportunity abroad, financial benefits and long travels.

Example 12

The following chart belongs to a native serving in the Indian Revenue Services as Income Tax Commissioner at Mumbai.

Native born on 23rd August, 1970

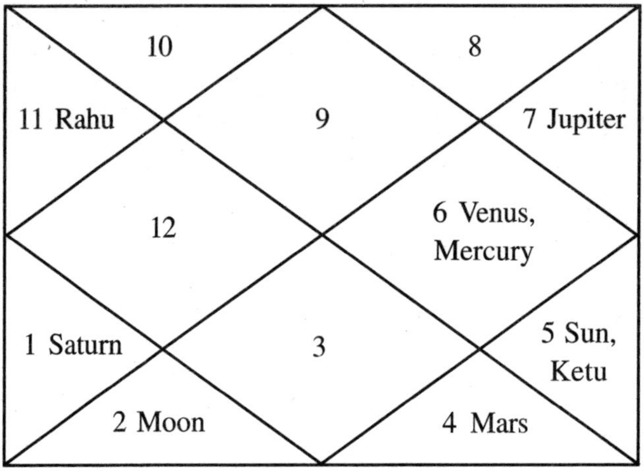

Discussions

The above chart is a unique example reflecting how friendly and good aspects can help build one's career and take the native to the top of success. The native's debilitated Mars is sitting in the 8th house and aspects Jupiter sitting in the 11th house. In fact, Mars rules the 5th house in the above chart and Jupiter owns the ascendant besides the 4th house. ***Thus, the exchange of aspects between the owners of the 5th and the ascendant has played most of the game in favour of the native. Mars provides strength to the ascendant and Jupiter aspects the 5th house, enabling the native achieve success in his projects.*** Besides, the owner of the ninth, Sun, is sitting in its own house and is conjunct with Ketu. Although the Sun's being conjunct with Ketu may bring early disappointments but the Sun is one of the strongest planets in the solar system. As such, Ketu cannot restrict providing benefits to the native, as it sits in a highly beneficial house.

Besides, the owners of the 10th and the 11th houses are conjunct in the 10th house, which form a strong Raj Yoga. ***In view of that the reader must keep in mind that when the native gets success, it is not one planet only that helps, but jointly good aspects and good placements of the planets working together to provide benefits to the native. In the above case Mars, Jupiter and Mercury as well as Venus have been greatly instrumental to provide benefits to the native who is currently working as a deputy Commissioner in the Income Tax Department.***

Bibliography

1. Campbell, Elizabeth Rose (2003) Intuitive Astrology; New York: Ballantine Books.
2. Cox, Kathleen; (2000); Vastu Living; New York: Marlowe & Company Publication.
3. Editors-Time-Life Books(1990)Mysteries of the Unknown: Cosmic Connections; Virginia: Time-Life Books
4. Gerwick-Brodeur, Madeline and Lenard ,Lisa; (2003); The Complete idiot's Guide To Astrology; (2003); New York: Alpha Books
5. Goldschneider, Gary (1994), The Secret Language of Birthdays; Middlesex, England: Penguin Books.
6. Huntley, Janis; (1998); Astrology; London: Element Publication.
7. Lewis, James R., (1994) The Astrology Encyclopedia, Detroit Washing, D. C. : Gale Research Inc.
8. Martine, Joanna Woolfolk; (2001) The Only Astrology Book You Will Ever Need: Madison Books: New York; Lanham.
9. Parashar, A. P. & V. K.; (2005), Explore the Power of Astrology; New Delhi: Unicorn & Pustak Mahal Publication
10. Parker, Julia & Derek (2000); Guide To Astrology; London: Dorling Kindersley Publication.

11. Parker, Julia & Derek (1991) Parkers' Astrology: New Edition; London: A DK Publishing Book.

12. Snodgrass, Mary Ellen (1977) Signs of The Zodiac; London: Greenwood Press

13. Tester, Jim, (1987) A History of Western Astrology; New York: Ballantine Books.

14. The American Astroanalysist Institute, (1976) Astroanalysis: The Capricorn Personality; New York: Berkley Books. Analysis .

15. William W. Hewitt, (1991) Astrology for Beginners; St Paul: Llewellyn.

16. White, Suzanne, (1986), The New Astrology; New York: St. Martin's Press

Books Consulted

17. A.P. Parashar & V.K. Parashar, (2004), Explore the Power of Astrology; New Delhi, Unicorn Publication (Pustak Mahal).

18. Krishna Ashant (2001), Lagna Darshan; Part One to Part Four; Delhi: Shila Lekh.

19. Rajendra Dhameza, (2003) Navans Phaladesh; New Delhi: Sobhagya Deep Prakashan.

20. Ramesh Upadhya, (2000), Jotish Tatva, Vivek, Datia: Shree Peetamber Peeth.

21. Sothida Mannan, (2000), Predicative Stellar Astrology; Chennai: Krishman & Co.

22. Suresh Chandra Mishra (1996), Brihat Parashara Hora Sastram; New Delhi: Rajan Publication.

Appendices

Appendix-I

Houses of a Horoscope

The area of the birth chart between the Earth at the center and the surrounding ecliptic is divided into sections called houses. There are twelve houses, and unlike the twelve signs of the zodiac, which revolve around the chart, the house positions are fixed. In the chart opposite and in those on the following pages, the houses occupy twelve equal segments of 30 degrees each, calculated by what is known as the Equal House System. Any of about twenty other systems may be employed to determine the size of each house, but the Equal House is the oldest method-dating back to the time of Ptolemy-and the easiest to use.

The houses are numbered, starting from the ascendant-always the beginning, or cusp, of the first house-and proceeding counterclockwise. The descendant is always the cusp of the seventh house. Each house represents an arena of everyday experience, such as career, family, and community standing. As the positions of the planets are plotted on the chart, a number of the celestial bodies will appear in certain houses, enabling the astrologer to determine the particular life situations is in which the planets influence supposedly will be felt if no planets appear in a house, however, it does not mean misfortune for that area of life or a lack of importance or interest. People who have children, for example, do not necessarily have planets in the fifth house, which governs offspring. The lack of planets may simply mean their lives are not defined by children. In addition, the houses are said to correspond to the different signs of the natural zodiac. The first house is thought to be imbued with the characteristics of Aries, and so on. Although on any given - individual's chart other zodiacal signs will typically fall within the houses and impart their own special qualities, astrologers claim that these natural traits are always present to some degree. The third house, for example, is said to govern communication and is influenced by inquisitive, logical Gemini. But, say astrologers, if someone's chart has the sign of Leo in the third house, the person would still be inquisitive; the style of communication would simply take on the essence of Leo, becoming more daring and flamboyant.

The areas of life thought to be affected by the houses, and the signs corresponding to each house, are examined below.

1 The first house, also the rising sign, corresponds to assertive, adventurous Aries. This house allegedly affects what is unique about an individualtemperament, disposition, appearance, and level of self-awareness--and influences all forms of outward behavior.

2 This house, relating to stable, conservative Taurus, reveals what is important or of value to a person. It governs moral values and money and possessions of all kinds, including attitudes toward them, how they are acquired, and how they are used.

3 The style and manner of communication, including speech and writing, are ruled by the third house, which corresponds to curious Gemini. Also governed are sibling relationships and short journeys.

4 The fourth house, influenced by nurturing and domestic Cancer, reveals an individual's homeboth the childhood abode and the adult home. It represents how one seeks or views security and also has a bearing on parents, particularly the mother.

5 This house, governing creativity, corresponds to artistic, warmhearted Leo. The fifth house also rules children, pets, all objects of one's affection, and pleasures such as holidays, the arts, sports, and gambling.

6 Work and health are said to be ruled by the sixth house, which is colored by the analytic sign of Virgo. Service to the community and attitudes toward subordinates are also included in this house.

7 The seventh house affects an individual's feelings about close relationships-not only emotional pairings but working partnerships as well. Libra's drive for connectedness influences this house.

8 The entire life process of sex, conception, birth, and death outlined by the eighth house and influenced by the dedicated arid ntensely emotional sign of Scorpio. This house governs attitudes about reincaniation, magic, and the occult, as well as the money or investments of others and the inheritance of possessions or traditions.

9 The ninth house is the house of religion and philosophy. it relates to the wanderer, Sagittarius, and rules extensive journeys of the mind, spirit, and body and the desire to explore outside one's own culture. This house governs higher education, publishing, languages, and the law, and it also reflects the drive to organize information into systems.

10 Ambition and desire for a standing in the community are revealed in the tenth house. Influenced by pragmatic and aspiring Capricorn, this house also governs parents, particularly the father and his relationship to work.

11 The eleventh house influences a person's creativity in social situations and interaction with individuals and groups. Corresponding to freethinking Aquarius, this house rules general hopes and dreams as well as political activity.

12 The twelfth house relates to self-sacrifice, service to others, and the need for seclusion. It also encompasses all forms of confinement-in hospitals, monasteries, prisons, or other institutions and privacy in terms of the unconscious, dreams, hidden problems, and secret enemies. The twelfth house is influenced by sensitive, vulnerable Pisces.

Appendix-II

Natural planets and natural signs in their houses.

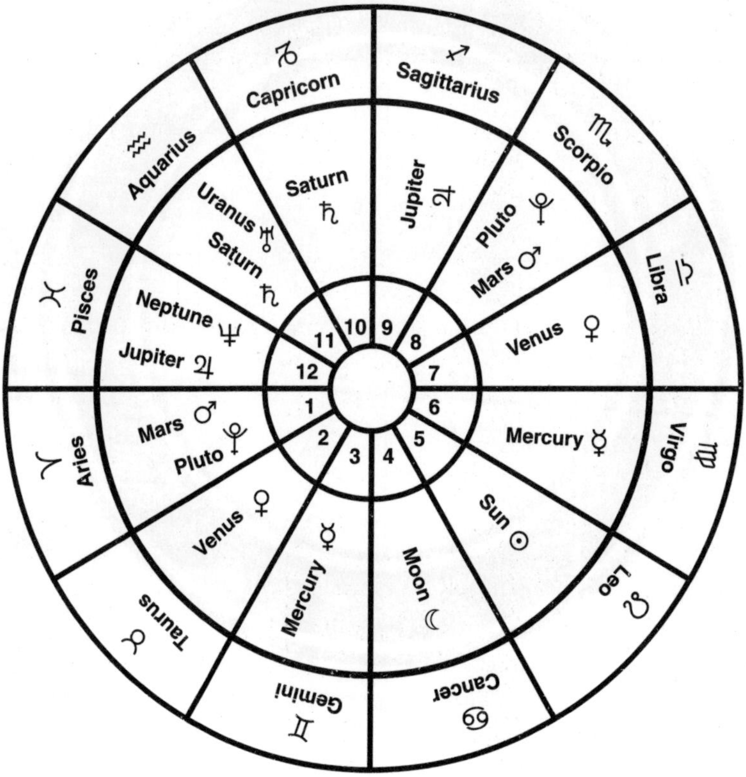

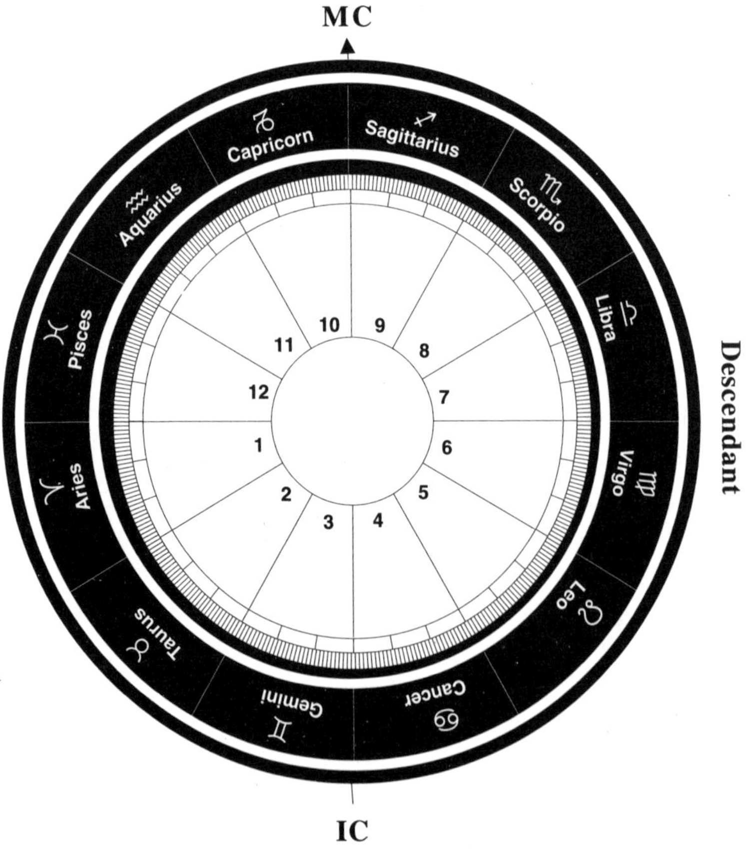
MC
Capricorn
Sagittarius
Aquarius
Scorpio
Pisces
Libra
Descendant
Aries
Virgo
Taurus
Leo
Gemini
Cancer
10
9
11
8
12
7
1
6
2
5
3
4
IC

Refining the Signs

According to traditional astrology, each sign of the zodiac has certain: intrinsic characteristics or, tendencies. Some of these attributes are said to derive from the planets; since each sign is allegedly ruled and thus influenced by one or more 'heavenly bodies (pages 34-37). Other traits are thought to be the result of the sign's connections to an element of nature (three, zodiac signs, called the triplicities, are said to correspond to each of the four elements) or to one of three qualities (four zodiac signs, or quadriplicities, are thought to relate to each quality).

The elements of nature are fire, earth, air, and water. Each sign is associated with an element, beginning with the designation of Aries as a fire sign and continuing in twin counterclockwise around the zodiac: Taurus corresponds to earth, Gemini to air, Cancer to water, and soon (opposite):

The fire signs-Aries,. Leo, and Sagittarius are described as enthusiastic, spirited, and impulsive, They are thought to be adventurous and innovative, yet impatient and at times impractical. Taurus, Virgo, and Capricorn are earth signs and are said to, be practical, logical, dependable, and way: They are also associated with the amassing of wealth, food, and creature comforts. Air signs Gemini, Libra, and Aquarius are associated with communication, reflection, and the application of ideas. They show a concern for possibilities, for what could be. And Cancer,

Scorpio, and Pisces, the water signs, are thought tai be sensitive, imaginative, private; and, compassionate.

They are said to show interest the intangible and a concern with dreams and the unconscious when in erpreting a birth chart, one of an astrologic first tasks is totally up the number of planets appearing in the fire, earth, air, and water signs. in some charts, planets may dominate only one element, but that situation is rare-most chants show a balance of two or three elements: A fire-water combination, for example, can be an intriguing mix of fire's enthusiasm and energy with water's imagination. Tempered by the presence of earth signs or communicated through air signs, this combination could be exceedingly powerful, according to astrologers. On the other hand, they say, those with a predominance of earth-water signs maybe practical and affectionate but lack the intellectual or emotional sparks provided by air or fire signs.

Some astrologers will advise clients with seemingly imbalanced charts to literally make contact with the element of nature-to seek heat or sunshine, for example, to counter a lack of fire signs. They also may recommend association with other people whose charts are abundant in the desired elements: The earth-water person allegedly tends to be introverted and to be overwhelmed. by details associating with air and fire people might lighten this individual's mood and perhaps spark creativity. As shown by the chart on the opposite page each house is also related to an element: The influence of the houses is considered more subtle than that of the signs, although an individual lacking planets in earth signs, for example; might; compensate for this deficiency with planet in the second house, which is considered an earth-related house. To add an additional level of information to the birth chart, each sign is also associated with one of three quadriplicities, ties or qualities. Said to influence the individual's relationship to the environment, the quadruplicates are known as cardinal, fixed; or mutable; and each imparts a particular essence to four signs. The cardinal signs-Aries, Cancer, Libra, and Capricorn-are considered exuberant, outgoing, and energetic; these

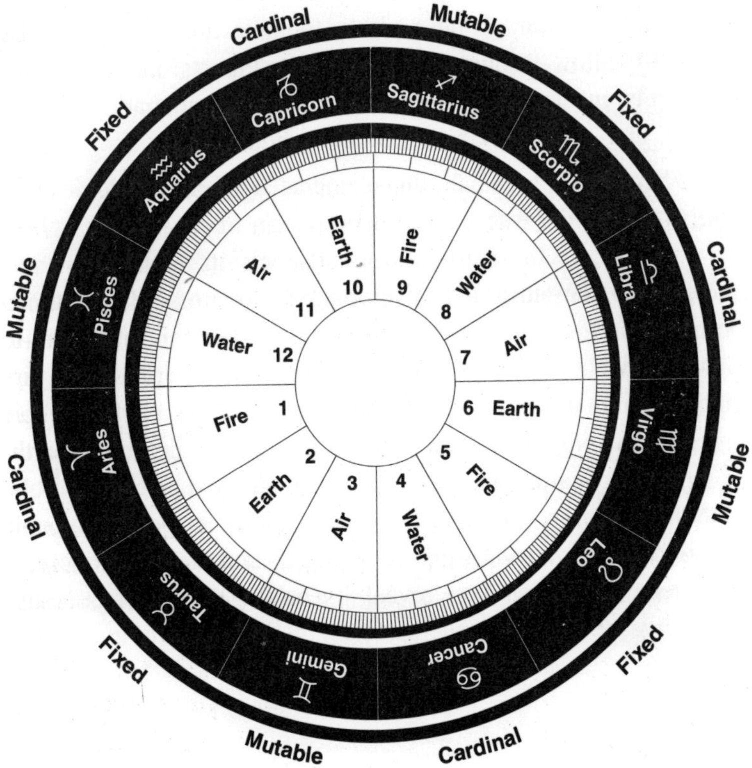

Cardinal
Mutable
Fixed
Cardinal
Mutable
Fixed
Cardinal
Mutable
Fixed
Cardinal
Mutable
Fixed
Capricorn
Sagittarius
Scorpio
Libra
Virgo
Leo
Cancer
Gemini
Taurus
Aries
Pisces
Aquarius
1 Fire
2 Earth
3 Air
4 Water
5 Fire
6 Earth
7 Air
8 Water
9 Fire
10 Earth
11 Air
12 Water

signs initiate action and take command. The fixed signs-Taurus, Leo, Scorpio, arid Aquarius-reflect stability, resolve, and resistance to change. They consolidate the ideas and actions of the cardinal signs. It is left to the mutable signs of Gemini, Virgo, Sagittarius, and Pisces which signal flexibility, adaptability, and communication-to take those ideas out into the world.

The houses, too, are classified as either cardinal, fixed, or mutable. Cardinal houses supposedly represent the initiation of new plans or projects; fixed houses are stabilizing influences for the implementation of those plans; mutable houses provide the ability to follow through on the project. Planets are said to act assertively in cardinal houses, become more emphatic in fixed houses, and more variable in mutable houses.

When taken together, the elements and quadriplicities are said to reveal the true nature of each sign of the zodiac. Aries, for example, is fire-cardinal and channels its enthusiasm and energy into initiating and developing future possibilities; those born under this sign are entrepreneurs, leaders, and innovators. Cancer is water-cardinal; this sign exhibits its enterprise through emotions and intuition. Sagittarius is fire-mutable, and focuses its energies on communication, perhaps through broadcasting, travel, or teaching; Sagittarians may also, at times, find release in fiery outbursts. Taurus, an earth fixed sign, gains its power through consolidation or stewardship of wealth or material goods. Leo; a fire-fired sign, is said to reveal its power through passionate creativity.

Appendix-IV

Retrograding Planets

Retrograde planets are not bad as commonly thought of. Just as humans need to retreat once in a while to renew their energies, so do the planets. When a retrograde planet is placed in a chart at the time of one's birth, it simply means to reconsider the functions associated with that planet. Should one consider it bad? Perhaps one should not. Once if an individual understands what one should do with that planet or what kind of advantage one should take from that retrograding, the individual can certainly take advantage of that situation.

When planets retrograde everyone experiences that retrograding. It means the retrograding planet is off on its treat. As such, the energy from the planet will feel 'different', though it is not quite such that we could pinpoint. For example, if Mercury is retrograding while it is transiting in one sign, it would mean that there might be communication break down. When a planet retrogrades, it is closer to the Earth than usually it is. Therefore, its energies are more intense. It is because of that that the energies from the retrograding planets require more efforts to be integrated. Sometimes the energy is reversed but sometimes it is intensified. But regardless of that, it is not just the same as usual. Let us keep in mind the following when any retrograding planet is transiting (placed) in a house in our chart and follow the advice.

The Sun and the Moon never retrograde. The Sun, unlike the other planets, does not follow any orbit but rather it is the point around which other orbits spin. The Moon revolves around the Earth and, therefore, does not follow any orbit. When Mercury retrogrades, we should feel encouraged to redo our things that we had not done before or not done correctly. It may also mean that our communication or expression becomes difficult and so we should try to put new efforts to redo it. When Venus retrogrades that would mean that during retrograde one should reconsider and re-evaluate everything one loves and to whom one loves. A transiting Jupiter indicates that it is the right time to grow internally and prepare oneself for opportunities that will be available when Jupiter goes direct. It is especially important to possess better awareness at that time to determine whether something offered to one is what one really wants. Accordingly, one should plan for the period when Jupiter goes direct. Let us take Saturn's retrograding. Saturn is the planet of systems and organization. When it retrogrades, it is the time to reconsider these things and discover methods and ways to improve them and to make them function better. Mars is the planet associated with action. As such, when Mars retrogrades, it indicates to check one's inward action. The main purpose of Mars's retrograde would mean to re-examine what motives one possesses and whether those motives are correctly thought of. Therefore, it is the time to determine whether one is on the right path or that path needs to be revised.

Salient features of Indian Astrology

—Prof. U.C. Mahajan, M.A., M.Phil

Humans are always curious about their future. Astrology is one such time-tested science that throws light on one's past and also predicts that unseen future which is clearly visible to those who correctly understand the various centuries-old interpretations. We may err but Astrology never goes wrong.

- **What does the Sun in the first house signify?**
- **Why is Jupiter in Aries benefic?**
- **What is meant by 'malefic' aspects?**
- **When will I get married?**
- **Why should I wear an emerald?**
- **Why do I suffer from recurring eye troubles?**

Find the answers to these and more, for it is all there in our respective horoscopes. This book provides a simple yet comprehensive approach to the study of the stars and planets, their placements, good and bad implications, and suggested remedies. The author further claims that doctors too have started acknowledging the efficacy of healing through astrological charts.

Go ahead. Cast your horoscope and find out what the stars have in store for you—in the present as well as in the future.

Demy Size • Pages: 160
Price: Rs. 96/- • Postage: Rs. 15/-

Explore the Power of ASTROLOGY

—Dr. A.P. Parashar
Dr. V.K. Parashar

Backed by years of astrological experience, Dr Ambika Prasad Parashar and his son Dr Vinod Kumar Parashar offer a fresh perspective on each Sun sign and the signs of other planets when they transit different houses in a chart (*kundali*). Examining the main areas of life – relationships, finances, family, career, health, love and personal characteristics – the authors probe the gifts of the Sun signs interwoven with the influence of other planets' aspects and transits in the houses. The book tells readers how things operate in life due to astrological influences, so that they can approach life from a new perspective to discover the right vocation and attain great success, happiness, love and peace. Case studies of prominent persons are dealt with extensively to help readers understand the planetary influences and other signs that indicate foreign travel, property, love, money, position, luck and other factors in life. The book also throws ample light on how to compute one's own *lagna* (rising sign) and make one's own chart, if required.

Demy Size • Pages: 200
Price: Rs. 96/- • Postage: Rs. 15/-